The Myth of Individualism

The Myth of Individualism

How Social Forces Shape Our Lives

Second Edition

Peter L. Callero

ROWMAN & LITTLEFIELD PUBLISHERS, INC.
Lanham • Boulder • New York • Toronto • Plymouth, UK

Published by Rowman & Littlefield Publishers, Inc.
A wholly owned subsidiary of The Rowman & Littlefield Publishing Group, Inc.
4501 Forbes Boulevard, Suite 200, Lanham, Maryland 20706
www.rowman.com

10 Thornbury Road, Plymouth PL6 7PP, United Kingdom

British Library Cataloguing in Publication Information Available

Library of Congress Cataloging-in-Publication Data

Callero, Peter L.
The myth of individualism : how social forces shape our lives / Peter Callero. -- Second Edition.
pages cm
Includes index.
ISBN 978-1-4422-1744-7 (hbk. : alk. paper) -- ISBN 978-1-4422-1745-4 (pbk. : alk. paper) -- ISBN 978-1-4422-1746-1 (electronic)
1. Individualism. 2. Conformity. 3. Culture. I. Title.
HM1276.C35 2013
302.5'4--dc23
2012044458

Contents

Preface to the Second Edition

Four years after publication of the first edition of this book, America's preoccupation with the question of individualism seems to have grown even more muscular. Evidence of its strength was in full view during the 2012 U.S. presidential election when President Obama gave a speech in Roanoke, Virginia, that included the following declaration:

> If you were successful, somebody along the line gave you some help. There was a great teacher somewhere in your life. Somebody helped to create this unbelievable American system that we have that allowed you to thrive. Somebody invested in roads and bridges. If you've got a business, that—you didn't build that. Somebody else made that happen.

On the face of it, this is not an unreasonable assertion. The problem, however, is that it flies in the face of many Americans' commitment to the ethic of self-reliance and independence—especially when it comes to the entrepreneurial spirit of small business owners. For this reason, Mitt Romney's campaign immediately pounced on Obama's statement, charging the president with a form of cultural treason. Within days, the Romney organization had produced bumper stickers, buttons, and posters asserting, "Government didn't build my business, I did," while television ads featured offended business owners who testified that their own economic success was indeed the result of hard work and independent initiative.

This book is intended to take us beyond the political rhetoric to explore in detail the specific ways in which social forces contribute to the lived experience of individuals. It does not deny the power of individuals to make decisions that have some effect on their own lives, but as sociologists know, this is only part of the story. The emphasis of this book is on the inherent sociality of the human species, our essential interdependence, and our fundamental need for interpersonal solidarity.

In this second edition, I have updated relevant statistical data and added new supporting references where appropriate. I have also extended the chapter on collective action to include analyses of both the Wisconsin Uprising and the Occupy Movement. But the most significant addition to the second edition is an entirely new chapter on the power of mass media. Here I review the historical development of the public sphere, explore different types of media influence, and examine particular issues of sex, violence, and politics.

American's distinctive faith in self-reliance and independence is a deep-rooted cultural conviction. For this reason, politicians and campaign strategists are quick to leverage its force to their advantage. But the truth is, Americans are like people everywhere, naturally social, interdependent, and shaped by social forces. This was the message of the first edition and remains the defining theme of the second edition.

Acknowledgments

When the actress Kim Bassinger gave her Academy Award acceptance speech in 1998, she displayed unique sociological awareness in her gratitude by thanking "everybody I have ever met in my entire life." It was a joke, of course, but it hinted at something many us know to be true: no individual accomplishment, creative or otherwise, can be disconnected from one's prior life experience.

Given that this book is about the myth of individualism, a similar open-ended proclamation of thanks is certainly in order. But recognizing the wide breadth of our interdependence and the seemingly endless list of our social contacts does not mean that some people aren't more important and influential than others. The individuals who have made distinctive contributions to this book are named below.

Jeremy Tanzer, University of Portland, read an early draft of the first edition and conducted a "test drive" by adopting a prepublication copy of the book in two sections of his introductory sociology course. His generosity and timely feedback have been invaluable. Michael Schwalbe, North Carolina State University, inspired this work with his successful advocacy of a "sociologically examined life," and provided detailed comments that improved the clarity of my prose and gently challenged hasty or undocumented assertions. Michael (and his students) also offered many excellent suggestions for changes that have been incorporated into the second edition of the book. Similarly, my colleague Dean Braa, Western Oregon University, has been both an informal editor and a font of motivation. It is safe to say that Dean's vociferous commitment to critical pedagogy has provoked this book into existence. Frank Frohmherz, Portland State University, also reviewed an early draft of the first edition and offered a constructive critique from the perspective of an academic activist. As founder of the Pacific Center for Global Justice, Frank is the epitome of public sociology. I am also grateful to my father, Dr. Vern Callero, who was the very first reader of the draft manuscript. His "outsider's point of view" was both helpful and humorous.

The second edition of *The Myth of Individualism* has benefited tremendously from suggestions made by several instructors who assigned the book to their students. This list includes Ray Pence from the University of Kansas; Ted Thornhill, St. Olaf College; and John A. Kovach, Chestnut Hill College. Others who read parts of early drafts or have shaped my sociological thinking in significant ways include my colleagues at Western Oregon University, especially Steve Gibbons and Maureen Dolan; participants in the regular "special seminar"; my children, Nicholas, Emilia, Patrick, and Samuel Callero; my mother, Diane Callero, and the rest of the Callero 16; and, of course, my students, especially those whose stories are shared in this book. I thank you all.

The editorial and production staff at Rowman & Littlefield has been efficient and professional. Sarah Stanton solicited feedback on the first edition and ushered me through a timely completion of the second edition. I am especially grateful for Alan McClare, who was the first to recognize the potential value of this nontraditional text. Alan also solicited professional reviews from Rosemary Powers, Eastern Oregon University; Susan Wortmann, University of Nebraska, Lincoln; and Peter Collier, Portland State University. Their critical feedback and editorial suggestions forced me to confront some limitations of structure and content.

Finally, I dedicate this book to Kathleen DeFuria Callero, the most influential presence in my life and the most beautiful reminder that life cannot and should not be lived alone.

Introduction

Production by an isolated individual outside society . . . is as much of an absurdity as is the development of language without individuals living together and talking to each other.

—Karl Marx

This inner isolation of the individual . . . forms one of the roots of that disillusioned and pessimistically inclined individualism which can even today be identified in the national characters and the institutions of the peoples with a Puritan past.

—Max Weber

When the U.S. Constitution was written in 1787, it established a historic set of legal principles that served the political interests of its authors—a small minority of white, property-owning men. Women, slaves, Native Americans, immigrants, and those who did not own property were not allowed to vote, could not be elected to office, and were denied basic human rights and liberties. As a consequence, approximately 90 percent of the inhabitants of the United States of America were not considered "persons" from a legal perspective. This narrow view of personhood still dominated in 1858 when even Abraham Lincoln argued that "there is a physical difference between the white and black races which I believe will forever forbid the two races living together on terms of social and political equality."[1]

A century later, the international debate over the legal rights of persons had shifted dramatically. In 1993, the Great Ape Project was founded as an organization of scientists and philosophers committed to conferring moral and legal rights to chimpanzees, gorillas, and orangutans. In the words of one of the organizations leaders, "The chimpanzee is an intelligent being, sociable, who knows how to live in society, who learns easily, who copies several techniques from others, who loves, hates, feels, and who appreciates advances and civilization, liking humans in spite all the tortures and suffering they have been through."[2] A committee of the Spanish parliament found itself in agreement with the Great Ape Project when in 2008 it passed a resolution that would extend some "human" rights to apes.[3]

The issue was further complicated in 2005, when the U.S. patent and trademark office rejected an application from a scientist who had invented a technique for merging human embryo cells with cells from the embryo of apes and other animals with the goal of creating a human-animal hybrid, or chimera. In explaining the controversial decision issued by his office, John Doll, a deputy commissioner for patents, said, "I don't think anyone knows in terms of crude percentages how to differentiate between humans and nonhumans."[4]

For hundreds of years humans have struggled with the question of personhood. Are women, slaves, and blacks equal to white men? Where is the line separating apes from humans? What criteria should we use to define an individual? For most of us these appear to be simple questions with obvious answers. They may even seem trivial queries unworthy of our time and energy. But in fact, the question of personhood has been one of the more significant issues in the history of human civilization. The way we choose to define an individual person has immense consequences for how we live our lives. Our religious beliefs, our politics, our legal system, and our economy are all based on particular beliefs about the individual. Anthropologists tell us that the answer to the question of personhood is very different from one culture to the next. Historians have demonstrated that within a particular culture the answer has changed rather dramatically over time. And today, if you were to ask your neighbor or friend for their definition of a person, there is a very good chance that the answer would be quite different from your own. Indeed, one need only examine the contemporary debate over abortion to appreciate the point.

This book addresses the question of personhood from a sociological perspective. To be more precise, it explores the relationship between the individual and society. From a sociological point of view one cannot define the individual without first considering the fundamental role of social relationships. In fact, for sociologists the individual and society are simply two sides of the same coin and cannot be separated. This means, for example, that our parents, siblings, coworkers, friends, and classmates are not only influential and important individuals but also actually a part of who we are. The merging of the individual and the social is also true of larger groups and institutions such as churches, businesses, schools, neighborhoods, and even nation-states. In other words, our very identity is a social creation that is constantly sustained by social relationships both small and large. Some of our social relationships are experienced as close and intimate, while others are experienced as more distant and anonymous, but all combine to make us persons.

This is not a common point of view. Most people today view personhood from a psychological perspective where the individual and society are assumed to be distinct entities. Take a moment and reflect upon the beliefs and assumptions you hold about your own self. If you are typical of most Americans you probably believe that an individual is a person with an independent and distinct identity. You may also believe that your true self is inherently unique and separate from others around you, or that society in one form or another works against your quest for personal freedom and individuality. While there is an element of truth to all of these statements, sociologists offer compelling evidence that the individual and society are one in the same, mutually supportive, and necessarily intertwined. The fact that most of us believe otherwise is evidence of a powerful cultural myth—the myth of individualism.

Of course, not everyone is equally committed to this narrow view of personhood, but research indicates that the myth of individualism is both widely held and growing in its influence—especially in the United States.[5] This is a troubling development because, as we will see later in the book, the myth of individualism causes serious social harms. For this reason it is ironic to note that the myth of individualism actually has a noble and honorable history.

The origins of common belief systems are difficult to track down. This is especially true of general ideas like *individualism* that have multiple roots tracing back more than two thousand years to ancient Greek civilization. Still, many scholars believe that our modern commitment to individualism took hold in eighteenth-century Europe during a period that came to be known appropriately as the Enlightenment.[6] It was during this time that the first smoldering coals of democracy were being stoked. The dominance of the monarchy and the superiority of the church were being challenged by both elite intellectuals and long-suffering serfs. Throughout Europe and America, new scientific disciplines were confronting superstitions, and centuries-old traditions of authority and control were collapsing. There was an emerging hope in progress toward a better future and a belief in the idea that people acting collectively could make the world a better place. Liberty was the watchword of the day. In this historical context, individualism was positive. It was synonymous with freedom and independence from oppression. In the words of Alexis de Tocqueville, the French aristocrat famous for his studies of American democracy, "*Individualism* is a recent expression arising out of a new idea. Our fathers knew only the word *egoism*. . . . Individualism is democratic in origin, and it threatens to develop as conditions equalize."[7]

Today, however, individualism has revealed a dark side that threatens to eclipse the very light of freedom and equality for which it once stood. Leaders of corporations and international finance employ the myth of a radical individualism to justify economic inequality. Lifestyles characterized by social isolation and loneliness are often defended as expressions of individualism. And "liberty" for many Americans now means protecting one's freedom to shop, purchase, and consume. Individualism was once an idea in support of altruism and collective emancipation, but it is now more closely linked to egoism and selfishness.

WHAT WENT WRONG?

When World War II came to an end in 1945, people across the globe reacted with a mix of joy, relief, and dismay. There was joy and celebration in the victory of the allied forces. The German Nazis, the Italian Fascists, and the Japanese nationalists were defeated, and it appeared that democracy had prevailed. Families around the world expressed a collective sigh of relief that the killing had stopped and the surviving soldiers were coming home to a more secure and peaceful world. But behind the joy and relief there was also a deep sense of shock and dismay over the massive scale of death, destruction, and torture that had been unleashed by military leaders on both sides of the battlefield.

In total, close to sixty million people were killed! Even more shocking was the realization that most of the victims were civilians—not active members of the military. More than six million Jews were *"efficiently"* exterminated and intentionally tortured by a government that had been democratically elected by the German people. Massive bombing campaigns of civilian neighborhoods in Europe were employed as a deliberate tactic by war engineers on both sides of the conflict. And in the United States, a democratically elected government came to the decision that it was morally justifiable to drop atomic bombs on two Japanese cities, instantly killing 150,000 civilians, maiming thousands more, and exposing the entire region to cancer-producing radioactivity that would continue to kill and deform for another generation.

How could this have happened? From where did this capacity to kill on such a grand scale originate? Is human nature inherently evil? Are we destined to forever repeat such horror? Can new forms of governance be used to control the violence? What about science and technology? Will we use these tools to produce more lethal weapons of mass destruction, or can we harness the same resources to improve health and prosperity across the planet? In the period immediately following the war these questions haunted citizens across the globe. And as politicians, scientists, artists, theologians, and other intellectuals debated the issue, an introspective world searched for answers.

In 1948, three years after the end of the war, two influential books were written in the context of this cultural soul searching. Both are science fiction novels that describe a future society where life is expertly planned and tightly controlled. And both are indicative of the mix of despair and hope that followed World War II. One story is full of optimism and describes a near-perfect utopia; the other is a frightening portrayal of control and domination in a world of fear and paranoia.

Walden Two, written by B. F. Skinner, tells the story of a radical thinker and fast-talking intellectual named T. E. Frazier who has established an experimental community in a relatively isolated locale of rural America. The narrative follows the visit of a skeptical college professor and his curious friends who have come to investigate the new community. As Frazier leads the guests on a tour, we learn that Walden Two is a relatively self-sufficient commune and home to roughly one thousand adults and children who appear to enjoy an idyllic life in a modern utopia. Instead of living isolated from each other in separate homes, the people of Walden Two enjoy a communal lifestyle where dining, child rearing, and work are shared. The social structure of the community is highly egalitarian with little variation in status, and the economy is so efficient that workers spend only fours hours a day in labor. As the story unfolds, we gradually learn from Frazier that the success of Walden Two is the result of behavioral engineering. The social expectations and cultural values of traditional societies have been rejected as a guide to the good life. Instead, the social planners of Walden Two have turned to the psychological theory of behaviorism for answers. According to behaviorism, human action and emotion can be controlled and redirected in positive ways by manipulating "contingencies of reinforcement"; which is another way of saying that positive behavior is rewarded. Using a strict scientific protocol on the infants and children of Walden Two, the community is able to extinguish all negative emotions, including jealousy and competition. There are no fences, jails, or law-enforcement personnel, and residents are free to leave. But why would they? It turns out that Walden Two is a genuinely peaceful, happy, and healthy place to live. In the end, freedom and dignity are preserved, and a good society is sustained by using the science of psychology to emancipate individuals from the negative forces that have corrupted other societies.

George Orwell's novel, *1984*, paints a far different picture of the postwar world. At the time this novel was written, the year 1984 was thirty-five years into the future, and the book served as a stark warning of a nightmarish society that lay ahead. The protagonist of the story is Winston Smith, a middle-aged government bureaucrat who lives alone in a dreary apartment in London, which is now part of the region known as Air Strip One in the powerful nation of Oceania. Winston is depressed, simmering with anger, and growing increasingly frustrated with his life in Oceania.

In this futuristic world there is one powerful organization, known simply as the Party, which monitors and controls all public and private affairs in the country. Winston is a member of the Outer Party, which means he is not part of the ruling elite. The methods of surveillance and manipulation are extensive and include the use of advanced electronic technologies, covert spying, propaganda, and torture. The city is plastered with posters of the Party leader that read "Big Brother Is Watching You," and most rooms have a *telescreen* that simultaneously propagates messages from the Party and records conversations and actions. Personal records of the past are forbidden, and the Party has rewritten history to conform to its interests. Perhaps most sinister of all, the English language has been replaced by *Newspeak*, which has the effect of altering memories, changing thought structures, and inducing compliance.

If any form of rebellion is detected, citizens are "reeducated" using physical and psychological torture. Despite these forces of intimidation, Winston is not deterred. He decides to take major risks by executing seemingly minor acts of resistance—keeping a diary, engaging in a sexual affair, and arranging a meeting with a Party leader who may also be secretly rebellious. Unfortunately, however, Winston's resistance is too weak and in the end the Party apparatus effectively quashes his struggle to be free. Nevertheless, the reader is left with one very dim ray of hope for the future. Oceania is divided into three classes, the Inner Party, the Outer Party, and Proles. Even though the Proles are in the majority, they pose no threat of revolution since they are uneducated and highly disorganized. Like animals, they are left alone and not closely monitored. But as Winston notes in a famous passage from the novel,

> If there was hope, it must lie in the proles, because only there, in those swarming disregarded masses, eighty-five per cent of the population of Oceania, could the force to destroy the Party ever be generated . . . if only they could somehow become conscious of their own strength, [they] would have no need to conspire. They needed only to rise up and shake themselves like a horse shaking off flies. If they chose they could blow the Party to pieces tomorrow morning. Surely sooner or later it must occur to them to do it.[8]

I was required to read both *Walden Two* and *1984* in a high school English class. I can't recall the exact year, but it was sometime between 1969 and 1971. This was a period in American history of great social upheaval. Massive protests against the war in Vietnam were occurring throughout the country, the civil rights movement was confronting racism and social segregation, a new consciousness regarding equality for women and environmental protection was spreading, and idealistic young people were actively searching for a more meaningful lifestyle, one less dominated by materialistic values and economic competition.

Although *Walden Two* and *1984* were reactions to the disruptions of World War II, both novels seemed to speak to many of my generation. Some of us could recognize the dangers of a government that limited personal freedom and used the military and police to suppress public protest. But others also believed a better world was possible—one more harmonious and peaceful than the present. Within this context the novels appeared to be contradictory—one described a dream utopia and the other a nightmare dystopia. B. F. Skinner was optimistic about the potential value of human scientific knowledge, but George Orwell warned of the dangers of bureaucratic and technological control. *Walden Two* implied that happiness was to be found in a society that was planned and controlled from the top by intellectuals, while *1984* hinted that emancipation could only come from the collective power of an ignorant and oppressed people working together.

Even though both books were obvious works of fiction, I often wondered if either one was an accurate picture of a future society. And by implication, which story was based on a more precise view of personhood? Are we destined to live forever in a world of war, hunger, sickness, poverty, and social inequality, or is a better world possible? Can progress be made through planned collective intervention? What political system is most fair and just? Can science serve as a tool for emancipation? It was later, when I went to college, that I discovered that these very issues were the ones that were being addressed in the discipline of sociology.

THE PROMISE OF SOCIOLOGY

This book is intended to serve as an introduction to sociological thinking. It is not, however, meant to be a comprehensive overview of the discipline. There are plenty of thick textbooks that serve this function well. Instead, my focus is on what I believe to be the defining concern of sociology, namely, *the relationship between our personal lives and the social forces that structure society.* This particular concern has been famously articulated by C. Wright Mills (1916–1962), one of the most influential American sociologists of the twentieth century. In describing what he called *The Sociological Imagination*, Mills argued that human liberation begins with understanding the relationship between "personal troubles" and "public issues."[9] Unemployment, for example, is no doubt a personal trouble for the individual who can't find a job. And if he or she were the only jobless person in the entire society, we might be justified in concluding that it is *only* a personal problem. But unemployment is never isolated. It follows a pattern and affects millions of people in an economy. In this sense it is a public issue and must be understood in terms of larger political and economic structures. The same can be said for many other personal troubles—divorce, illness, and crime are all experienced as troubles in the context of one's personal life, but each is also a matter of public concern at the level of "social structure." And importantly, changes in personal life are often caused by structural changes—forces beyond the control of a single individual.

Once after giving an introductory lecture on sociology I was approached by an obviously anxious student who demanded to know if sociologists hold to the belief that "society controls individual behavior." When I answered "No," the student looked relieved and said, "So individuals control their own future." Again I answered "No." Clearly frustrated, the student insisted on a straight answer. "It has to be one or the other; it can't be both! Now which one is it?" Over the years I have found that many students approach sociology from a similar perspective. There is a tendency to believe that an understanding of the individual-society relationship boils down to a simple distinction: either our personal actions and choices shape our life or something called "society" is the master of our destiny. But this is a false choice that oversimplifies human behavior, much like the nonsense debate of "nature versus nurture" or "psychology versus biology." The real world is more complicated. The answer to my student's question is that we are both free to act on our choices *and*, at the same time, very powerful social forces shape us.

Karl Marx (1818–1883), one of the founders of sociology, put it best when he said, "[People] make their own history, but they do not make it as they please; they do not make it under self-selected circumstances, but under circumstances existing already, given and transmitted from the past. The tradition of all the dead generations weighs like a nightmare on the brains of the living."[10]

In other words, the decisions we make and the actions we choose to take are made under conditions that we inherit from generations that came before us. In this way, social forces rooted in the past shape our options in the present. As we will see in the following chapters, social forces come in many different shapes and sizes and affect us in ways that are very often undetectable. Some are found in culture, some in the economy, others impress upon us in the immediate situation, while still others are found deep in our psyche. All, however, have a history that originates with generations before us. The first step toward a better world is in identifying these forces and distinguishing between the good and the bad, those that limit our dignity and freedom from those that enhance cooperation and justice. The science of sociology can help us in this quest.

Political solutions cannot succeed if they are based on false assumptions, prejudice, and intolerance for diversity. Nor can they work if they are forced on us through political, economic, or military power. Reasonable and effective solutions must be arrived at democratically, aided by a social theory that has been tested using systematic observations and careful analysis. I do not believe a perfect world is possible, and sociology does not promise a utopia. There is no Walden Two in our future (and even if there were, it certainly wouldn't come to us through behaviorist psychology). But I do believe that progress toward a better society can be achieved. Working collectively we can avoid the Orwellian nightmare. Indeed, history is a testament to the triumph of democratic resistance. In the United States, for example, we have seen the abolition of slavery, women have achieved greater equality with men, child labor has been mostly eliminated, and civil rights have been extended to a greater number of people. On the international stage we have seen the defeat of the apartheid system of racial discrimination in South Africa, totalitarian regimes have collapsed in many nations, and the value of democracy is increasingly recognized. Still, immense challenges remain. As I write this, acts of genocide have left more than four hundred thousand dead and another one million homeless in Darfur, Africa. The United States continues to occupy Iraq and Afghanistan by military force, and the specters of global warming and nuclear war threaten the very survival of the planet.

Sociology alone cannot solve these public issues. But sociology can play a very important role. The promise of sociology is *enlightenment*—not religious or spiritual enlightenment, but intellectual enlightenment; where reason triumphs over myth, science over superstition, and democracy over political domination. The path to intellectual enlightenment is often a personal struggle that requires courage, the courage to confront long-held beliefs and traditions in a quest for truth. But if light is to triumph over darkness, we must be prepared to challenge comfortable ways of thinking, and we must never fear to examine new ideas—no matter how threatening. In the famous words of the great eighteenth-century philosopher Immanuel Kant (1724–1804),

Sapere aude!

(Dare to know!)

Chapter One

Individualism

The Power of a Myth

> Man is the more vulnerable to self-destruction the more he is detached from any collectivity, that is to say, the more he lives as an egoist.
>
> —Emile Durkheim [1]

When Theodore John Kaczynski was born on May 22, 1942, his parents, Turk and Wanda, were likely filled with joy and hope for their firstborn child. Growing up in the Chicago suburb of Evergreen Park, Ted gave his family every reason to be proud. His academic performance in elementary school was so advanced that he skipped the sixth grade. While in high school he was identified by teachers as a brilliant student, demonstrating superior skills in math and science. In a letter of recommendation to Harvard University, his high school guidance counselor wrote, "I believe Ted has one of the greatest contributions to make to society. He is reflective, sensitive, and deeply conscious of his responsibilities to society."[2] Most who knew him as an adolescent described Ted as being somewhat quiet and a bit shy. No one expected him to one day become one of the FBI's most wanted criminals.

By the age of twenty, Ted had graduated from Harvard and was enrolled in a doctoral program in mathematics at the University of Michigan where he worked as a teaching assistant. Students and faculty alike gave him positive evaluations, describing him as "one of the best students I have ever taught," "first rate," and "enormously impressive."

In 1967 Ted received his PhD in mathematics after completing an award-winning dissertation on "Boundary Functions." That same year, his reputation as a brilliant mathematician landed him a job as an assistant professor at the University of California, Berkeley. At the age of twenty-five Ted Kaczynski was fast becoming an academic superstar.

As a young man, Ted's outward demeanor was neither deviant nor countercultural. If anything, he appeared more conservative and traditional than other people his age, often wearing a coat and tie on the Berkeley campus during a period when the "hippie" movement was in full bloom. For this reason, his colleagues at Berkeley were shocked when, after only two years as a professor, Ted resigned his position to leave academia behind for good. He would never again teach mathematics or hold a professional job of any kind.

From 1969 to 1977 Ted drifted between odd jobs and survived on savings and limited financial assistance from his parents. In 1971, after borrowing money from his brother, he purchased a small plot of land outside of Lincoln, Montana, in the Rocky Mountains just west of the Continental Divide. Here, in a relatively remote region bordered by national wilderness areas, Ted built a very rustic one-room cabin. The wood-framed building was very small—only ten feet by twelve feet in size—and looked more like a tool shed than a home. It had no indoor plumbing or electricity, and an old cast-iron, wood-burning stove kept the cabin warm during the cold Montana winters.

It was in this near wilderness location, halfway between Yellowstone and Glacier National Parks, that Ted pondered his place in the world, developed his own personal critique of modern society, and wrote his "manifesto"—a rambling political manuscript that called for revolution and identified science and technology as the enemy. It was also here that he initiated his bloody campaign of revenge.

The violence was at first relatively weak and directed at local intruders. He took potshots at oil company helicopters and broke into a neighbor's house where he smashed chain saws, motorcycles, and snowmobiles. Then in February 1978 he constructed his first homemade bomb. It was a crude device built inside in a long, narrow box with an experimental fuse that was designed to explode when opened. Writing in his journal at the time, Kaczynski remarks, "Of course, I would like to get revenge on the whole scientific and bureaucratic establishment, not to mention communists and others who threaten freedom, but, that being impossible, I have to content myself with just a little revenge."

Because the bomb was too big to fit into a postbox, it had to be hand delivered to its target. So Ted boarded a Greyhound bus, traveled to Chicago, and placed the explosive package near several cars on the campus of the University of Illinois, Chicago Circle. He had hoped to kill someone working in the science and technology buildings. The bomb, however, was a dud.

Kaczynski, was undeterred, though, and soon returned to the drawing board. Within a year he had constructed another explosive device; this one was smaller, more powerful, and, more importantly, it worked. A graduate student at Northwestern University's Technological Institute was hospitalized with lacerations and facial burns when he opened a cigar box found on campus.

But Kaczynski was still not satisfied, and a journal entry records his lament that the victim did not "suffer any permanent disability." Six months later he constructed a third bomb using gunpowder and a barometer, and sent the package to an address that required airmail—his target, a passenger jet. The bomb exploded as designed, but American Airlines Flight 444 was able to land safely, barely averting a major catastrophe.

Over the next sixteen years Ted Kaczynski would deliver sixteen more bombs. With each one the explosive power and technological sophistication improved with scientific precision. His targets included university students and faculty specializing in science and technology, employees of airlines and airplane-manufacturing companies, computer store staff, and leaders of the logging industry. The FBI would dub him the "Unabomber" in recognition of his early targets—universities and airlines. A total of twenty-three individuals would be seriously injured by Kaczynski's explosions. Three people would die. Kaczynski's final victim was Gilbert Murray, the president of the California Forestry Association, headquartered in Sacramento. When a curious-looking package arrived at Murray's office suite on April 24, 1995, his coworkers joked that the parcel might be a bomb. The threat, however, was not treated as serious. Murray was alone in an inner room when he cut through the brown paper and string covering the small wooden box. The resulting explosion tore through the building and was so powerful it nearly disintegrated Gilbert Murray's body. At the time of his death Murray was forty-seven years old, a husband, and father of two children.

A reward of $1 million was established for information leading to the identification and apprehension of the Unabomber. However, in the end it was Ted Kaczynski's younger brother, David, who was responsible for the arrest. On June 24, 1995, exactly two months after killing Gilbert Murray, Ted Kaczynski mailed an anonymous manuscript to the *New York Times*, *Washington Post*, and *Penthouse* magazine. The lengthy, 3,500-word document was titled "Industrial Society and Its Future," and in it Kaczynski described in academic detail his sociopolitical philosophy, his revolutionary motives, and his justifications for the attacks. Ted Kaczynski now had a worldwide audience for his private musings. David Kaczynski's wife was the first to suspect that the author might be Ted, and she convinced her husband to speak to authorities.

On April 3, 1996, the FBI surrounded Kaczynski's cabin and arrested him without incident. A seventeenth bomb was found inside his simple home. On May 4, 1998, following a highly sensational trial, Theodore John Kaczynski was sentenced to life in prison without the possibility of parole. He is presently incarcerated at the U.S. Penitentiary Administrative Maximum Facility—a "supermax" prison in Florence, Colorado.

TED KACZYNSKI AS RADICAL INDIVIDUALIST

Most commentators attempting to "make sense" of the Unabomber have focused on telltale signs of a madman who gradually succumbed to a debilitating mental illness. News stories recounted the fact that Ted's father had committed suicide in 1990 while suffering from a terminal disease. Some analysts pointed to a family life with overwhelming pressure to succeed as a cause of Ted's alienation and rage. Others claimed that Ted's experience in college was to blame. After all, wasn't it at Harvard where he was exposed to a philosophy of moral relativism and was the subject of an experiment in the psychology department? Ted's mother shared with reporters her belief that Ted's deviance could be traced to infancy and the time he was hospitalized for a case of hives at nine months of age. Still others suggested that the spirit of the 1960s was the culprit and that radical environmentalism had polluted his thinking. Ted Kaczynski, himself, vigorously defended his sanity and argued that all of the attempts to define him as ill were aimed at discrediting his political philosophy.

So how do we make sense of Ted Kaczynski? While there may be good reason to believe that he suffered from a mental illness, this is not the focal point in a sociological perspective. Sociologists are less concerned with the psychological particulars of a single individual's life and are more interested in the larger pattern within which a life is led. In other words, sociologists focus on the social context that gives meaning to one's action. It is not just the biography of the individual but also the history of the society within which the individual lives that is of greater importance. In the case of Ted Kaczynski, this means we need to see him less as a madman and more as a person who reflects something about his society. So what does the Unabomber tell us about our society? What does his notoriety tell us about this moment in history? And what do his thoughts and actions tell us about ourselves?

I offer the story of Ted Kaczynski as an illustration of someone who personifies in both thought and action the life of a radical individualist. That is to say, he is someone who exhibits an extreme and deviant commitment to the myth of individualism. As noted in the introduction, the idea of individualism has been around for quite some time, and intellectuals have been writing about the concept with much gusto since the European Enlightenment of the seventeenth and eighteenth centuries. There are also a number of relatively recent books that address the topic in one form or another, focusing on specific aspects or limits of individualism.[3] As a consequence there are many different uses and definitions of this term.[4] I combine many of these points of view in the following description: individualism is a belief system that privileges the individual over the group, private life over public life, and personal expression over social experience; it is a worldview where autonomy, independence, and self-reliance are highly valued and thought to be natural; and it is an ideology based on self-determination, where free actors are assumed to make choices that have direct consequences for their own unique destiny.

I recognize that there is a lot of information crammed into this long-winded definition. Over the rest of this chapter we will take the time to carefully unpack and examine the meaning and implications of its various component parts. For now, it is enough to recognize that on the surface, individualism doesn't sound so bad. In fact, many readers may see in this definition a highly desirable moral framework or ideology that matches up nicely with their own point of view. Indeed, it is safe to say that individualism is one of the most dominant values in American society. Some would even say it is the defining characteristic of American culture. So it should come as no surprise that Ted Kaczynski, born and raised in Middle America, should adopt an individualist philosophy. What makes Ted Kaczynski so intriguing as a terrorist is not that he was violently opposed to American values but rather that he is in fact an extreme American, someone who represents an expression of American values on steroids! In his lifestyle, in his political philosophy, and in his acts of terror he represents the principles of individualism in excess. In this way, the story of the Unabomber provides insight into American society.

By way of analogy, compare two imaginary snow skiers. The first skier has little experience and is traveling down a very short run. She is physically unfit, has slow reflexes and poor eyesight, and as a result crashes into a tree at slow speed, spraining a knee. The second skier is an Olympic champion. She is in superb physical condition and is moving downhill as fast as anyone in the history of the sport. Near the end of her lengthy run she loses control and crashes into the very same tree. The accident results in many broken bones and a long hospital stay. The first skier is incompetent, and her collision was due to a failure to master the mechanics of the sport. The second skier is exceptionally skilled but suffers a much worse fate because she had "mastered" the sport. Think of Ted Kaczynski as the second skier. His story is a warning about the dangers of hyperindividualism where cherished American values of independence, self-reliance, freedom, and privacy are out of control, over the top, and in the end very destructive.

Kaczynski's extreme commitment to individualism is evident in (1) his intentional avoidance of personal relationships, (2) his deliberate physical separation from others, (3) his belief that he could live out his life completely independent of a larger community, (4) his solitary development of a personal program of social reform, and (5) his private strategy to unilaterally impose his ideas through a series of violent acts that destroyed the lives of others.

Again, it is important to recognize that modest expressions of individualism can be beneficial and constructive. There are times, for example, when social isolation can facilitate self-reflection and a sense of inner peace. But when one's everyday life is intentionally amputated from family, friends, and neighbors in the manner of Ted Kaczynski, isolation can be personally harmful. In the same way, we can recognize the value of a self-sufficient student or employee capable of independent work. But in the case of Ted Kaczynski, self-reliance also meant an uncompromising rejection of others' beliefs and a steadfast refusal to cooperate. Kaczynski sought to reform society on his own terms by eliminating the threats that he personally identified. He was not interested in democratic deliberation or the development of common interests. Freedom of choice and self-determination are virtuous principles, but when selfish individual interests threaten to destroy the common good, the limits of individualism are exposed.[5]

A CULTURE OF INDIVIDUALISM

When I was a graduate student at the University of Wisconsin in the early 1980s, my wife and I lived in a large student-housing complex reserved for families with children. The two-story building that included our apartment was designed around a common green space that incorporated a sandbox and play area for children. When the weather was warm enough, the families would gather in this area to barbeque, play a little Wiffle ball, and share stories. It was a culturally diverse neighborhood where the sounds of many different languages mixed with the dinnertime aroma of an international market. Our section of the complex included families from Iceland, India, Mexico, Indonesia, Iran, and several countries in Africa. On one particular summer day while relaxing in our little park, my wife and I were surprised to see another parent gently scolding our three-year-old son, Nic. I don't recall the details of Nic's "offense," but I do remember thinking that he probably deserved to be reminded about "playing nice." However, at the same time I couldn't escape feeling a little angry at the sight of another adult "parenting" our child. I remember thinking to myself, "Mind your own business! Why aren't you looking after your own kids?" Besides, I hardly knew this person, who acted like the neighborhood mother hen. I had learned earlier that she and her husband were newly arrived from Nigeria and that she had several young children of her own, but that was about it. My frustration didn't end with this one incident. Over the course of the next several weeks I was shocked to discover that the children in the same Nigerian family were often left "unattended" in the common play area. It was as if the new arrivals expected the rest of us to supervise their children. It would be one thing if we had been asked to babysit, but this never happened. To make matters worse, the Nigerian children would "borrow" the other kids' toys without permission. If another child's Big Wheel tricycle was not being used, they would simply hop on and ride around as if they were the owners.

Looking back, I can see that there are two possible interpretations of my neighborhood experience. First, one could argue that the mother from Nigeria was both overbearing and irresponsible when it came to child care. She was obviously sticking her nose into other people's business, while at the same time failing to supervise and control her own children. This was my preferred interpretation at the time, and it left me feeling superior and self-righteous. There is, however, another explanation for the events. The young Nigerian mother may have been acting in a very responsible and caring manner according to the values and practices of her culture. Think of the well-known African proverb, "It takes a village to raise a child." Within a more communal approach to child care, other adults in the village or neighborhood are expected to share in the duties of parenting. From this point of view, disciplining a neighborhood child and expecting others to look after one's own children is actually responsible behavior. This can also explain why the Nigerian children would "share" and "borrow" toys in a more generous manner. In a communal culture, the distinction between "mine" and "yours" is less clear. In my initial reaction I was interpreting the events from my own cultural perspective, one that places more emphasis on individualism. But in Nigeria, independence and individualism are not as highly valued. We can see this in the results of an international survey of values. In 2000, when a representative sample of adults in Nigeria was asked to identify qualities that children should be encouraged to learn, only 26 percent mentioned "independence." But when the same question was asked of a sample of adults in the United States a year earlier, 61 percent mentioned "independence."[6]

American society is saturated with the holy waters of individualism. Our literature, music, film, and television praise and celebrate those who succeed as individuals, especially if they go it alone against all odds. We are inspired by the "rags to riches" stories of the underdogs who start with nothing and succeed by "pulling themselves up from their bootstraps." Some of these stories are mythical (Rocky Balboa) while others are very real (Oprah Winfrey), but all have the same effect of affirming individual self-reliance, determination, and hard work against all social barriers. It is in many ways the sacred American dream, and it is a value system that is reinforced in many subtle but ubiquitous ways. Take the following aphorisms that most of us have either heard or have spoken at one time or another:

"You have no one to blame but yourself."

"God helps those who help themselves."

"Think for yourself."

"Look out for number one."

"No one can make you feel inferior without your consent."

"Give a man a fish and you feed him for a day. Teach a man to fish and you feed him for a lifetime."

"Know thy self."

"Genius is 1 percent inspiration and 99 percent perspiration."

These common sayings are part of a larger cultural story or narrative that we use to make sense of the world, to make our points in an argument, or to legitimate a plan of action. They sound like good advice mostly because they are familiar. They are, in this sense, taken-for-granted truths that usually go unquestioned.

The same themes of self-reliance, independence, and individual responsibility are found in the children's stories we pass down from generation to generation. Consider the story of the *Little Red Hen*. When she finds a grain of wheat and asks for help in planting, harvesting, milling, and baking, all of her barnyard friends refuse to lend a hand. For this reason we learn that she is justified in eating the bread "all by herself" and not sharing with her friends who turn out to be lazy loafers. A similar principle is reinforced in the classic version of the *Three Little Pigs*, where the two brothers who take the quick and easy route to building a house are eaten by a wolf who easily "blows the houses down." The third brother who labors away at building a brick cottage is able to survive, killing the big, bad wolf in a pot of boiling water as he descends from the chimney. The only surviving pig is the hero—smart, hardworking, well prepared, and, in the end, alone and brotherless. A different version of individualism is celebrated in *The Wizard of Oz*, where Dorothy is in a struggle to find her way back home to Kansas. Although she receives advice and assistance from her new friends and a charlatan wizard, it turns out that she was searching in the wrong place. All she needed to do was click her heals together; throughout her journey she had the power to save herself.

Scholars have demonstrated that the myth of individualism as a theme in literature can be traced back to the sixteenth and seventeenth centuries in Europe when the very first novels were ever written.[7] At that time, however, individualism was not celebrated. The now-classic characters of Dr. Faust, Don Quixote, and Don Juan were the original individualists. But in each of these stories the central character is punished for excessive egoism. Faust and Don Juan end up in hell while Don Quixote becomes the subject of ridicule. It is not until the eighteenth century, when the movements toward democratic governance, scientific knowledge, and religious independence were changing Western civilization, that we find positive images of characters acting as individualists. The story of Robinson Crusoe, written by Daniel Defoe in 1719, is the first to project a more favorable image of the hero separated from community. Crusoe is shipwrecked on an island but manages to thrive despite his isolation. It is interesting to note that in all four of these classic early novels, the hero is a single male whose only lasting relationship is with a more subservient male companion, a theme that is still very much evident today in popular American fiction. Think of the Lone Ranger and Tonto, Huckleberry Finn and Jim, Batman and Robin, Joe Friday and Bill Gannon (of *Dragnet* fame). In general, the classic American cowboy, hardboiled detective, and comic book superhero are widely recognized and often celebrated for their independence from the rest of us. From Clark Kent and Peter Parker to Adrian Monk and James Bond, American entertainment culture highlights the theme of success and salvation through the acts of individuals (usually men) who are in one form or another alienated or isolated from mainstream society.

Here it is important to recognize that the myth of individualism appears to be a more dominant trait in the fictional lives of American men—as opposed to American women. Think, for a moment, about the following pairs of traits and behaviors juxtaposed in columns A and B:

A	B
soft	hard
passive	aggressive
weak	strong
timid	brave
emotional	rational
gentle	rough

Which column would you say best describes a typical superhero? In which column would the word masculine more likely be found? Now ask yourself, in which column would you put the words independent and self-reliant? If you are typical of most Americans, you probably answered "column B" to all of these questions.

This brief exercise illustrates several things. First, it shows that stereotyped qualities of what it means to be male and female are often reinforced and popularized in fictional characters. Second, it also shows that the values linked to individualism are more commonly seen as male characteristics. This does not mean that men and women are inherently different along these lines, but it does suggest that images and stories in books, magazines, television, and film can reinforce our beliefs, values, stereotypes, and myths associated with individualism. In this way, Ted Kaczynski's bizarre life can seem strangely familiar. In many ways his philosophy and lifestyle are well-worn threads in the larger tapestry of American culture, especially the culture of the American male. Indeed, the lifestyle of Ted Kaczynski has eerie parallels to that of Henry David Thoreau (1817–1862), considered one of the most important authors in the history of American literature. For a period of more than two years, Thoreau retreated to a small, self-built cabin on a relatively isolated plot of rural land near Concord, Massachusetts. The experience of living a life of natural simplicity on the shore of Walden Pond was the inspiration for his classic memoir *Life in the Woods*. Like Kaczynski, Thoreau also attended Harvard, was a fervent environmentalist, and a passionate advocate of individual resistance to government and civil laws that violated his personal standards of justice. In his famous essay titled *On the Duty of Civil Disobedience*, Thoreau proclaimed, "The only obligation which I have a right to assume, is to do at any time what I think right." The difference, however, is that Thoreau's individualism led him to fight slavery and American imperialism with personal acts of peaceful resistance, while Kaczynski came to the conclusion that individual acts of violence and terror were the appropriate political solution.

This does not mean that classic American literature and popular entertainment do not at times celebrate themes in opposition to individualism. There are certainly many examples of characters who are considered evil antagonists because of their egotistical desire to succeed. We can all think of a classic story or two where the ideas of community, conformity, and collectivism are rewarded. The Frank Capra film *It's a Wonderful Life* is a good example of anti-individualism in American culture. John Steinbeck's novel *The Grapes of Wrath* is a very influential celebration of family and community solidarity; and in children's literature, Shel Silverstein's *The Giving Tree* presents a straightforward critique of selfish individualism. The point that I want to emphasize here is simply that the myth of individualism is a central and dominant dimension of American society. It is not, however, the only value or myth that characterizes our culture.

ECONOMIC INDIVIDUALISM

Earlier we defined individualism as a belief system that privileges the individual over the group, the private over the public, and the personal over the social. If this generalized faith in self-reliance and autonomy were found only in our books, bedtime stories, TV shows, and movies, it would be of very limited interest to sociologists. But in fact, individualism is much more pervasive. It is a guiding principle for many of our social institutions, affecting the way we live our lives in important ways. For example, Evangelical Christians forcefully assert that eternal salvation requires a personal relationship with Jesus Christ. Our educational institutions from grade school to college are structured to enhance individual achievement in a competitive system of evaluation. Even our professional athletic teams model individualist thinking as they compete to sign the top free agents to multimillion dollar contracts, challenging the oft-heard dictum that there is no "I" in "TEAM."

For sociologists, there is one form of individualism that is considered more important than any other, and that is the individualism that defines our economic system. In fact, many sociologists argue that the ideology of individualism emerged historically as a direct consequence of the rise of a capitalist economy. Still other sociologists argue that an individualist worldview was the starting point and that our modern economic system is in fact the effect of capitalism and not the cause. Setting this larger chicken-or-egg debate aside for now, the key point of consensus among sociologists is that the belief system we call individualism corresponds historically with the rise of a capitalist economic system.

Capitalism is the name we use to describe our present economic system. The basic principles of capitalism are rather simple and familiar but rarely examined.[8] First, a capitalist economy distinguishes itself from other economic forms in that it depends upon the idea of private property in the production process. This means that the things that we buy and sell in the market such as food, clothing, cars, homes, and so on, are produced in a process that is privately controlled. A relatively small number of individuals own the factories that produce our cars and computers; a small percentage of the population owns the land that grows our food and feeds our livestock; and the raw materials needed to construct our buildings and power our automobiles are held by a very wealthy elite. The vast majority of people in a capitalist economy do not personally own the means of production. For most of us, when we refer to private property we think of the consumer goods we have purchased from somebody else. So it is important to emphasize that the distinguishing form of private property under capitalism is not our personal items or the things we buy to consume; rather, it is the private property that is used to produce the things that we buy. Under capitalism the production of goods is privately owned and privately controlled, and the people who own the means of production are called capitalists. The most important and powerful capitalists are the ones who own and control very large businesses and corporations. Only about 1 percent of the population would fall under this category.

A second defining feature of capitalism is a labor market. Since most individuals under a capitalist system can't produce the goods they need to survive, they must find a way to secure food, shelter, clothing, and other essentials. For most people, this is accomplished by trading or selling one's labor to a capitalist; in other words, we must find a job. Capitalists are the primary purchasers of labor since they are the ones who own the factories, tools, and land. When someone is looking for a job in a capitalist economy, they are essentially searching for someone who will trade an ability to labor for a wage. If they are unsuccessful, they will be unemployed and without an income. In this way, survival becomes a personal responsibility of the laborer.

Finally, capitalism is characterized by the profit motive. Profit is the engine that drives the entire system, and it is the goal of every capitalist. The motivation to make a profit is not the same thing as the motivation to get rich, although the two are definitely related. Profit refers to the specific way that capitalists make money. If you are a capitalist, you make money by selling the things that your workers produce. If you can sell these products for more than they cost to produce, then you have made a profit. In this way, there is a motivation to keep production costs low, which usually means keeping workers' wages low. For this reason the history of capitalism has been characterized by a conflict between workers and capitalists. Under capitalism, big business owners and heads of major corporations are not motivated by a desire to employ many people, to make communities healthier, or to make the world a better place. Their first and foremost ambition is to make a profit, which is to say, accumulate capital. If this can be accomplished by moving a factory to another country, then that will be the goal. If there is profit in paying workers less than they might need to live a comfortable life, then so be it. Indeed, if a capitalist could find a way to produce goods and make a profit by substituting all human labor with machines, it would be celebrated.

Our capitalist economic system has become so dominant in scope and power that it is difficult for most people to imagine any alternative. Indeed, some people actually believe capitalism to be a natural expression of human nature! But sociologists disagree and emphasize the fact that economic systems are not natural. Indeed, from a historical perspective, capitalism is a very recent invention. It originated in Europe less than five hundred years ago when it gradually replaced feudalism. Most human civilizations have thrived for thousands of years without capitalism, and since there are many different ways to produce and exchange goods in a market, there is no doubt that future societies will likely construct alternatives to capitalism. But for now, capitalism reigns supreme.

More than any other economic system, capitalism has an individualist orientation and supporting philosophy. This should be evident in the requirement that the production process is privately owned as opposed to being held and controlled by some larger public entity such as a village, a tribe, or the people who have a hand in producing the products. Individualism is also evident in the idea of a labor market where a person's time and energy becomes a personal commodity and workers are assumed to be individually responsible for securing their own employment. But individualism is most blatant in the philosophical assumptions that most economists use to justify and defend capitalism.

INDIVIDUALISM IN ECONOMIC THEORY

Although there are different schools of thought about how economic markets operate, the theories that are used by most pro-capitalists today begin with the assumption that individuals act out of self-interest and that personal decisions are made so as to maximize private benefits. This point of view leads to the rather illogical conclusion that when all individuals act selfishly in the market, everyone benefits. Thus, pro-capitalist economists argue that when consumers buy the best products at the lowest prices they are rewarding the most efficient companies and putting pressure on other companies to improve their productivity or risk losing profit. This same competition is said to be good for the labor market where workers acting in their own self-interest are expected to move freely to businesses that pay higher wages and offer more benefits. The belief is that the more individuals are left alone without government intervention, the better the economy is for everyone. In this way, laws that limit the freedom of capitalists to do what they want in the market are considered bad for the economy. This position is known by the French term laissez-faire, which roughly translates as "leave it alone." Thus, the laissez-faire economists think a capitalist economy works best when it is uncontrolled and simply allowed to take its own course.

Government regulations that set minimum wages, require safe work environments, and established an eight-hour workday have been historically opposed by capitalists and laissez-faire economists. A major reason for their opposition is the belief that these laws limit business profit and violate the principle of radical individualism. Milton Friedman (1912–2006), one of the most influential economists and advocates of capitalism in the twentieth century, represents this position when he argues,

> The most reliable and effective protection for most workers is provided by the existence of many employers. As we have seen, a person who has only one possible employer has little or no protection. The employers who protect a worker are those who would like to hire him. Their demand for his services makes it in the self-interest of his own employer to pay him the full value of his work. If his own employer doesn't, someone else may be ready to do so. Competition for his services—that is the worker's real protection.[9]

In this quote we see evidence of the assumption that individual self-interest is the key motivating factor in economic relations. In fact, Friedman goes on to argue that people engage in all forms of social cooperation for the same selfish reasons. From his perspective human greed is the defining feature of every society. Again, in his words, "What kind of society isn't structured on greed? The problem of social organization is how to set up an arrangement under which greed will do the least harm; capitalism is that kind of system."[10]

From the point of view of sociology, Friedman is not completely wrong. Capitalist societies are influenced by greed, but not because greed is a natural and dominant quality of human behavior; rather, it is because capitalism promotes an individualist philosophy where self-interest is rewarded. In societies where capitalism is not the dominant political system, we do not find this same emphasis. Friedman is therefore wrong to assume that greed is the defining quality of human nature.

WHAT'S WRONG WITH INDIVIDUALISM?

The ancient Greeks were among the very first to organize their society around basic principles of democracy. The political systems of these early city-states were far from perfect, and many people were excluded from the privileges of citizenship. Nevertheless, we owe Greek civilization a debt of gratitude for demonstrating the potential of a political system that privileged a governing constitution, citizen representation in an assembly, debate, voting, and a jury system. It is interesting to know that within this democratic context, the Athenians had a specific name for someone who did not adequately meet their obligations as a citizen.[11] If you did not regularly participate in debate, if you demonstrated poor political judgment, and if you selfishly put your own personal interests ahead of the larger community needs, you were considered an idiot. Today we use the term idiot in a different pejorative sense, but the original meaning is instructive.

The individualist worldview, where autonomy and independence are believed to be natural and where personal interests are seen as superior to community interests, is in both the ancient Greek and modern American sense idiotic. This is shockingly obvious in the philosophy and life of Ted Kaczynski, but it is also true in a more subtle way for advocates of economic individualism such as Milton Friedman. In both instances supporters of a radical individualism are committed to the false dichotomy of self versus society. The idea that the person and the group are independent and completely distinct entities is a serious oversimplification of the relationship between one's self and one's society. In truth, the social world sustains our individuality as much as individuals sustain society. For this reason, being forced to choose between an individualist or a collectivist orientation is a bogus dilemma. This phony predicament is based on a mistaken understanding of personhood, and as this book will show, it is not supported by the empirical evidence. When false beliefs become widely accepted and begin to guide behavior in destructive ways, we can say the belief system is a myth. The artificial separation of the self from society, with the belief in the primacy and superiority of the autonomous actor, is the myth of individualism. Breaking this myth is a fundamental goal of this book.

One of the problems with a belief system characterized by radical individualism is that it promotes a narrow and limited understanding of freedom. Even though American political culture is especially associated with the twin concepts of freedom and liberty, our historical interpretation and application of freedom lacks consensus and consistency. Many of us learned in grade school that the Pilgrims fled Europe in search of religious freedom, but when the first European settlers found their freedom in the new land it was at the expense of native people who experienced domination at the hands of the American colonizers. Similarly, students are taught that the American Revolution was a war of independence from the tyranny of the British, but the historical record also reveals that many of our great patriots were not concerned with the tyranny they inflicted on their very own African slaves.

Clearly, one person's freedom can become another person's oppression. When the North and the South faced off in the American Civil War, both sides fought to defend liberty and freedom as holy causes. Abraham Lincoln was arguing for the emancipation of slaves when he wrote, "Those who deny freedom to others deserve it not for themselves; and, under a just God, can not long retain it."[12] But Jefferson Davis, the president of the southern Confederacy, also claimed to be defending freedom in his righteous assertion that "the tyranny of an unbridled majority, the most odious and least responsible form of despotism, has denied us both the right and the remedy. Therefore we are in arms to renew such sacrifices as our fathers made to the holy cause of constitutional liberty."[13] These two different interpretations of freedom were still being forcefully defended some one hundred years later during the civil rights movement. Writing from jail in Birmingham, Alabama, Martin Luther King Jr. was promoting organized civil disobedience when he declared, "We know through painful experience that freedom is never voluntarily given by the oppressor; it must be demanded by the oppressed."[14] But George C. Wallace, then the governor of Alabama, railed against recent civil rights legislation by defiantly proclaiming, "I am having nothing to do with enforcing a law that destroys your right—and my right—to choose my neighbors—or to sell my house to whomever I choose. . . . Let it be known that we intend to take the offensive and carry our fight for freedom across this nation."[15]

The same strong commitment and advocacy for freedom is very much evident today. In 2004, for example, then-president George W. Bush called on all Americans to support the "war against terrorism" by arguing that it is a battle to defend the very principle of freedom itself: "The terrorists are fighting freedom with all their cunning and cruelty because freedom is their greatest fear—and they should be afraid, because freedom is on the march."[16]

But despite President Bush's contrary claim, it is hard to identify anyone who publicly professes to hate freedom or despises those who love liberty. The truth is, most political leaders in the twenty-first century believe their organization or nation-state is acting in defense of freedom. Even Osama bin Laden, the former leader of the al-Qaeda terrorist network, used freedom to justify the September 11 attack on the United States:

> We fought with you because we are free, and we don't put up with transgressions. We want to reclaim our nation. As you spoil our security, we will do so to you. . . . Free people do not relinquish their security. This is contrary to Bush's claim that we hate freedom. Let him tell us why we did not strike Sweden, for example.[17]

Clearly, what is at issue here is not a belief in freedom or a commitment to liberty as a desirable value but rather some very consequential differences in the definition of freedom.

One way to sort through the competing conceptualizations of freedom is to distinguish between negative freedom and positive freedom.[18] Most of us think of freedom as the ability to do whatever we desire without the interference of someone else. For example, if someone locks you in a prison or threatens to kill you for speaking your mind, you are not free. If a government forces you to practice a particular religious faith or makes it illegal to obtain a formal education, you are not free. And we would all agree that someone who is bought and sold as a slave or who is otherwise restricted from participating in the political system is not free. We call this particular understanding of freedom negative because it focuses on the negative barriers that must be removed before a person is able to do what they want or be whatever they desire. This is the understanding of freedom that Governor George Wallace of Alabama was using when he argued against the new civil rights legislation that outlawed racial segregation in his state. It is also the definition of freedom that motivated Ted Kaczynski to physically isolate himself in rural Montana and to write in his "manifesto" that "one does not have freedom if anyone else (especially a large organization) has power over one, no matter how benevolently, tolerantly and permissively that power may be exercised." The problem with negative freedom, however, is that it is based on the myth of individualism and is therefore incomplete and unbalanced.

Positive freedom, in contrast, begins with the assumption that human action is inherently social and that real liberty requires more than the removal of barriers. Under positive freedom there is the additional focus on providing the resources that enable people to achieve or realize their full potential. For example, can we say that people are truly free to vote if there is no polling station within one hundred miles of their home? Are children truly free to receive a formal education if attendance requires unaffordable tuition? Does someone actually have free political speech if they have no access to a media platform? And can we say there is a right to life when health care necessary for survival is denied? Positive freedom emphasizes both the removal of barriers and the creation of a social context necessary for free action. This is the view of freedom that Martin Luther King Jr. was advocating when he criticized communism for its excessive social barriers and critiqued capitalism for its excessive individualism. "Communism forgets that life is individual. Capitalism forgets that life is social, and the kingdom of brotherhood is found neither in the thesis of communism nor the antithesis of capitalism but in a higher synthesis. It is found in a higher synthesis that combines the truths of both."[19] Positive freedom reminds us that our individual autonomy is wrapped up with the freedom and autonomy of others. One person's freedom to smoke can limit another person's freedom to breathe clean air and live a healthy life. One person's freedom to sell their house to anyone they please can limit another person's freedom to live wherever they please. And one person's right to hire and fire employees can limit someone else's freedom to work and earn a living.

Another problem with the myopia of individualist thinking is that it can limit our ability to locate solutions for our most challenging social problems. When we are committed to the myth of individualism, we fail to appreciate the fact that personal troubles are usually tied to social issues. When this happens we typically overemphasize "personal responsibility," "psychological therapy," or "individual skill development" as strategies for resolving troubling issues. By way of analogy, consider the following parable:

> Three friends are walking along a river bank when they notice a body floating downstream. Alarmed and moved by the sight, all three dive into the water to pull the victim to shore. Immediately after resuscitating the poor soul they notice another person floating downriver also in need of help. After saving the second drowning victim they see a third and then a fourth. At about this time one of the friends begins to run up river away from the scene of the growing emergency. Assuming that their colleague has panicked and is quitting on them, the two remaining friends call out in anger and frustration, questioning her self-serving actions: "Where are you going? Can't you see these people need our help? How can you quit now?" Ignoring the calls to return, the departing friend makes her way up river to a destination point that reveals precisely what she had anticipated. A high-traffic bridge crossing the river has collapsed; vehicles and pedestrians are falling into the swiftly moving current. Without hesitation she quickly erects a barrier that diverts traffic away from the bridge. [20]

In this story, the friend who ran upriver understood that the solution to the drowning problem was structural and that it required addressing the root cause of the problem. As long as her friends focused on the immediate task of pulling individual bodies from the river, there would be no end to the drowning problem. If the problem continued for some time, individualist solutions to the problem would likely emerge. For example, some people might advocate more swimming lessons in the community. Others might organize a counseling service to assist those who experienced the trauma of falling into the river. Still others would likely stress personal responsibility and a "sink or swim" philosophy that blamed the victims for their carelessness and failure to act with more caution. The point here is that an individualist perspective hinders the identification of structural solutions. Unless a more sociological orientation is achieved, effective resolutions to social problems will escape us.

There are numerous historical examples of collective solutions to public problems that have enhanced freedom and dignity of the person by changing the social structural conditions of society. The establishment of a democratic system of government and the abolition of slavery as an economic system are examples of collective action that have addressed the root causes of social problems. But as long as the myth of individualism is prominent in a culture, there are going to be leaders and interest groups who advocate for "individualized" strategies. We see this, for example, in public policy proposals that stress the "privatization" of public life and the unsubstantiated faith that the competitive forces of a "free market" will have universally positive benefits. We saw this perspective represented earlier in the economic individualism of Milton Friedman. This pro-capitalist economist supported the privatization of public parks, the selling of public forests, and even movement toward the privatization of public education. Ted Kaczynski, of course, represents the most radical individualist in this regard in that he not only supported the complete "abolition of the economic and technological basis of the present society" but also actively sought to bring about such a "solution" through his private acts of anonymous terror.[21]

In the final analysis, the myth of individualism may be most disruptive and unsettling in the way it legitimates social isolation and contributes to an increasingly alienated lifestyle. Sociologists have collected overwhelming evidence that community involvement, civic engagement, and social activity in general have been on a steady decline in the United States since at least 1970. Surveys show that Americans are 35 percent less likely to attend public meetings, 15 to 20 percent less interested in politics, and 25 percent less likely to vote today than we were forty years ago. During the 1960s, about 50 percent of all Americans spent some time as an active member of a club or organization such as the Elks, PTA, Knights of Columbus, or League of Women Voters. Today that number has been cut in half. Evidence of an increase in social isolation extends to our informal social connections as well. Over the past thirty years, there has been a 30 percent decline in "family dinners" and we are 45 percent less likely to "have friends over" for a social gathering. Even our participation in many sports has fallen by 10 to 20 percent since the 1980s. This includes traditional sports such as softball, tennis, and volleyball as well as sporting activities such as hunting, fishing, and camping. One exception is bowling, which is more popular than ever. However, even though the number of bowlers is up, the number of bowling leagues has dropped by more than 40 percent since 1970, suggesting that Americans are increasingly "bowling alone."[22]

In one recent study, sociologists examined changes in the size and intensity of interpersonal relationships over a twenty-year period.[23] Using data from two representative samples of Americans interviewed in 1985 and in 2004, they discovered that dramatic changes had occurred over this period. Almost three times as many people now say they have no one in their lives with whom they can "discuss important matters." Similarly, the average number of confidants (discussion partners) dropped from three in 1985 to two in 2004. Even more striking, in 1985 most respondents said that they had three close confidants, but in 2004 most respondents said that they had zero. The smaller size of close interpersonal networks is due to fewer confidential conversations with both friends and family, although the decline of friendship connections appears to be more serious. In general, the evidence indicates that Americans are rapidly losing contact with others, especially in our neighborhoods and other public places.

Once again, Ted Kaczynski is an extreme representative of the trend in American society toward greater social isolation. In an angry letter written to his family in 1991, he dramatically expressed his desire for isolation: "I have got to know, I have GOT TO, GOT TO, GOT TO know that every last tie joining me to this stinking family has been cut FOREVER and that I will NEVER have to communicate with any of you again."[24] For Ted Kaczynski, liberty is found in a solitary existence. But as we have seen throughout this chapter, this belief is a myth that may contribute to a less caring, less just, and less free society.

SOCIOLOGY AS MYTH BUSTER

Some readers may be familiar with *MythBusters*, the popular television show on the Discovery Channel. In this reality-based entertainment program, special-effects experts Adam Savage and Jamie Hyneman explore the veracity of extreme stories associated with the natural world. Over the years, the two amateur scientists have sought to determine whether or not a penny dropped from a skyscraper could kill an unsuspecting pedestrian, if radio signals could be transmitted through dental fillings, and whether an assassin could kill someone with a bullet made of ice. In a more recent episode they tested the urban legend that a construction worker falling from the top of a building was able to glide safely to earth because the piece of plywood that he was holding served as a sort of wing or parachute. Using human dummies and wood of various sizes and shapes, Savage and Hyneman were able to bust the myth of the flying man, demonstrating to the television audience at home that attempting such a feat on the job would likely result in death or serious injury.

In much the same way, social scientists employ systematic methods of observation and analysis to test hypotheses associated with the social world. In this sense, sociologists are also myth busters. By exposing beliefs and practices to the light of reason and by gathering relevant evidence, it is possible to debunk stereotypes, discredit prejudices, and demystify traditional acts of discrimination and domination. Race, gender, and class exploitation have all been systematically challenged by sociological research, and as a consequence, sociological findings have made significant contributions to greater equality and justice in the world. Today, fewer people believe in the superiority of a "white race," the intellectual inferiority of women is no longer assumed by a vast majority of the population, and the inherent laziness of poor people is widely rejected. Unfortunately, however, many destructive myths continue to endure, and bogus belief systems still legitimate unequal distributions of power and control. In fact, today we still find remnants of these historical prejudices among some community leaders and influential public figures.

In 2005, Lawrence H. Summers, then president of Harvard University, gave a presentation at a national conference where the focus was on the underrepresentation of women and minorities in science and engineering. In his speech he shocked the academic audience when he asserted that women were less likely to be scientists and mathematicians due in part to limitations in their "intrinsic aptitude." In his view, inherent differences in ability between men and women contribute to the dearth of female scientists. Also in 2005, Bill Bennett, the former secretary of education under President Ronald Reagan, surprised a radio audience when he said, "But I do know that it's true that if you wanted to reduce crime, you could—if that were your sole purpose, you could abort every black baby in this country, and your crime rate would go down." The implication here is that blacks are inherently more criminal and, as a logical consequence, eliminating blacks will reduce crime. And in 2004, Bill O'Reilly, the host of the FOX News show that bears his name, shared with the television audience his explanation for poverty in the United States. "It's hard to do it because you gotta look people in the eye and tell 'em they're irresponsible and lazy. And who's gonna wanna do that? Because that's what poverty is, ladies and gentlemen. In this country, you can succeed if you get educated and work hard. Period. Period."

In all three of these examples, you might recognize a common commitment to the myth of individualism. In each statement, the speaker assumes that patterns of social inequality are the result of physiological traits or psychological dispositions. Are they right or wrong? You may have an immediate gut reaction to either agree or disagree with Summers, Bennett, and O'Reilly. Your opinion may even be backed up by personal experience with women and math, or poor people and crime, but opinion and personal experience cannot settle the issue. A truly scientific answer must be based upon empirical evidence collected and analyzed in a systematic process that is publicly transparent and open to critique and revision. In the chapters that follow, we will review some sociological evidence that challenges individualist assumptions. We will also begin to identify the social forces that shape our lives.

Chapter Two

Becoming a Person

The Power of Symbols

If you prick us do we not bleed? If you tickle us do we not laugh? If you
poison us do we not die? And if you wrong us, shall we not revenge?

Many readers may be familiar with the famous quote that begins this
chapter. It is spoken by the character Shylock, a Jewish moneylender,
in William Shakespeare's *The Merchant of Venice*. In this passage,
Shylock is making an appeal for his humanity and the humanity of all
Jews. The play was written during the sixteenth century, a time in
Christian Europe when people of Jewish heritage were widely despised
and often portrayed as villains in popular drama. The culture of anti-
Semitism reflected in Shakespeare's play has a long history dating back
more than two thousand years. Obscene stereotypes and legal acts of
exclusion and discrimination have been used for centuries to minimize
the dignity and humanity of Jewish people. It is a pattern that continued
in Europe for more than four hundred years after Shakespeare and
culminated in the German Nazi's so-called final solution of the Jewish
question—what we know today as the Holocaust.

In the following sections we will take a closer look at two other
examples of dehumanization in American history. In both instances we
find groups of individuals who have been defined as *nonpersons* by
powerful forces in their community. The historical circumstances and
social categories are different, but the fundamental social processes at

work are the same—and in the end, the destructive consequences are dreadfully similar.

EVIL WITCHES

In 1692 a frightening crime wave swept through the New England colonial settlement of Salem Village. During a brief period from February to September, over two hundred men and women were arrested and held in prison under suspicion of practicing witchcraft. Twenty people would eventually be executed for their crimes, along with two dogs also suspected of being agents of the devil. This sudden furor of criminal activity occurred in a town with a total estimated population of six hundred.

The crime of witchcraft was not invented by the early colonizers of New England. Similar trials and executions had been occurring in Europe for over two centuries, and it is estimated by historians that over one hundred thousand men and women were prosecuted for witchcraft between 1450 and 1750. Of these, at least sixty thousand were eventually executed; most were tortured to death by being burned alive at the stake.[1] What was unique about the Salem area crime wave was that it represented a sudden spike in criminal activity that just as quickly reverted back to the lower rate of accusations and trials. To understand the nature of the crime and this particular crime wave, we need to appreciate the context within which it occurred.

The early colonizers of New England were for the most part religious zealots who believed that they were destined by God to establish a community in the New World that would be a model of Christian faith and practice. Most of these first immigrants were Puritans, who by today's standards would be considered radical religious fundamentalists. They fervently rejected the traditional rituals, sacraments, and ecclesiastical hierarchy of the European Catholic Church, which they viewed as promoting unnecessary and corrupt accoutrements of "popery."[2] For the same reason, many Puritans were dissatisfied with the Church of England for failing to more completely reject the theology and practices of Catholicism. The New England Puritans advocated a simpler and more "pure" form of Christianity that they believed to be more characteristic of the early church.

In their social practices, the New England Puritans rejected many "frivolous" forms of public entertainment. Similarly, musical instruments and artwork were eliminated from their worship services along with the traditional notion of a religious priesthood. Puritans also believed in predestination, the theological idea that God preordains some souls for salvation and others for damnation. Under this view, the grace of God is all that determines one's spiritual destiny, and neither good works nor free will can affect this ultimate outcome. Even though religious beliefs and civil laws were one and the same, this was a highly private and introspective religion. It could evoke deep feelings of anxiety and soul searching among believers who sought to determine whether they were one of the elect—predestined for heaven—or one of the damned—predestined for hell.[3]

It was within this strict religious context that Bridget Bishop found herself under suspicion in the summer of 1692. At the time, there was little doubt among the locals that Mrs. Bishop was deviant. She was on her third marriage—her first two husbands had died prematurely—and she was known to be loud and quarrelsome in public. In the eyes of the community, Bridget was no doubt a weak and sinful woman. But could she also be a handmaiden of the devil? The decision facing the townspeople of Salem was simple—they must determine whether Bridget Bishop was a person or a witch.

At her trial, Bridget was accused of entertaining "people in her house at unreasonable hours in the night to keep drinking and playing at shuffle-board, whereby discord did arise in other families, and young people were in danger to be corrupted."[4] She was also accused of wearing clothes that were extravagant and unreasonably delicate and colorful. But the most damning testimony was from neighbors and acquaintances who charged that Bridget possessed supernatural powers. Witnesses claimed that she had afflicted young children with uncontrollable fits and convulsions. It was also reported that she had caused a giant timber to crash from the roof of a Christian meeting house; and several accusers claimed that Bridget had appeared to them at night in the form of a spirit with evil intentions.

According to local mythology, if Bridget Bishop was a witch, there was a good chance that her body would display the telltale markings of a beast from hell. For this reason, a jury of women was instructed to strip Bridget of her clothing and stick pins into any suspicious looking spots on her body in search of evidence. It was during this examination that a "witch's teat" was discovered between her anus and her vulva. At the time, it was believed that these hidden teats were used to suckle small animal demons known as *familiars*. These rodent-like beasts were thought to provide assistance to witches in their evil undertakings. Despite Bridget's consistent and forceful denial of every charge, and despite the fact that her teat had "withered away" within hours of its discovery, the judge decided that Bridget Bishop was a supernatural being. On June 10, 1692, she was executed by hanging, the first death sentence in the infamous Salem witch hunts.

This particular episode of American history has received attention from social scientists for several reasons. First, it has proven to be a unique case study of how crime and deviance come to define the moral boundaries in a relatively homogeneous religious community.[5] Second, it offers a compelling illustration of how strong and assertive women have been demonized and punished in American society.[6] And most important for our purposes, it is an example of how an individual's claim to personhood can be rejected by the larger community. Bridget Bishop thought of herself as a person, but the powers that mattered decided otherwise. Why is it that we are not allowed to define our own humanity? Before exploring this question in some depth, let us examine one more historical example of how personhood has been challenged.

MISSING LINKS

One hundred and fifty years after Bridget Bishop was tried, convicted, and killed for the crime of witchcraft, Americans and Europeans turned their attention to a new category of "subhuman" deviants. They were called "missing links" and were believed to be a unique and rare animal species that represented an evolutionary stage connecting humans and apes.

During the two-century span bridging the seventeenth and nineteenth centuries, much had changed in the world. Political revolutions had dismantled the dominant religious power structures, and an emerging faith in science and technology was leading to a more rational view of the cosmos. Perhaps no single event had more influence in this radical shift than the publication in 1859 of Charles Darwin's *The Origin of Species*. In this scientific monograph, the origin and development of all life-forms was explained as an evolutionary process of *natural selection*. It would not be long before references to "genetic inheritance" and "survival of the fittest" entered the popular lexicon. The idea that our early ancestors were less than human was both startling and exhilarating. On the one hand, the unique and superior place of humans in the history of the planet was now being called into question. This was a revelation that put traditional religious explanations on the defensive and contributed to an emerging sense of anxiety about the nature of our human origins. At the same time, however, the possibility of "improving" humankind by manipulating natural laws of breeding was now considered a legitimate possibility by a growing number of people. This was the objective of the so-called *eugenics movement* whose adherents advocated selective birth control, sterilization, and laws controlling marriage and procreation as a strategy for reducing crime, improving intelligence, and eliminating the unfit from the gene pool. For the eugenicists, progress through biological intervention gave new hope for a better society.

It was in this context that Julia Pastrana garnered international attention. She was reportedly born in Mexico in 1834, and as a young woman was "purchased" by an American businessman who made a living by "exhibiting" her unique physical characteristics. We know today that Julia was born with *congenital hypertrichosis*, a rare condition characterized by a disproportionate growth of hair on all parts of the body, including the nose, forehead, and ears, as well as the torso, arms, and legs. In the nineteenth century, however, Julia was advertised as the "missing link" connecting apes and humans in the evolutionary chain. Thousands of curious spectators in the United States and Europe paid money to view the so-called baboon-human hybrid in an exhibit that toured until Julia and her newborn son died from complications of childbirth in 1860.

A similar life of public degradation awaited a tiny eight-year-old girl named Krao, who was "captured" in Siam (present-day Thailand) by a German explorer. From 1883 until around 1889, Krao was poked, twisted, measured, weighed, photographed, and otherwise analyzed and displayed by inquisitive scientists and unscrupulous promoters. Like Julia Pastrana, Krao was also born with hypertrichosis and was exhibited as an "ape-girl" at the Frankfurt Zoo in Germany. In one scholarly article published in the prestigious journal *Nature*, an anthropologist summarized his evaluation of Krao by concluding that she was living proof of a subhuman hairy race. Another prominent anthropologist concurred and speculated that Krao represented a species connecting Neanderthals and "civilized man"—the missing link. Until her death in 1926 at the age of fifty-one, Krao made a living in the Ringling Brothers and Barnum and Bailey Circus as the celebrated "Human Monkey."

Krao and Julia Pastrana are but two of a relatively large number of individuals who were categorized as human-animal hybrids or as representatives of a subhuman species. Many of these people displayed characteristics of hypertrichosis and made a living in the circus with such sensational monikers as "The Bearded Lady," "Jo-Jo the Dog-Faced Boy," and "Lionel the Lion Man." Others were "scientifically" dehumanized and exhibited as examples of an exotic subhuman "race" defined by skin color, unique body parts, facial characteristics, or overall size. Ota Benga falls into this category. A "pygmy" from the African Congo, Ota was enslaved and exhibited at the St. Louis World's Fair in 1904 and later at the Bronx Zoo in New York City. In both instances he was shown as an inferior species and was displayed next to apes. Reporting on the new exhibit, the *New York Times* noted, "The pygmy was not much taller than the orangutan, and one had a good opportunity to study their points of resemblance. Their heads are much alike, and both grin in the same way when pleased."[7]

The cases described here should not be dismissed as unique or aberrant products of unprincipled promoters. Rather, they should be viewed as illustrations of an authoritative interpretation of personhood that influenced social policy, politics, and scientific theories well into the twentieth century. The dehumanization of individuals based on physical characteristics was considered scientifically legitimate and politically popular. Organizations with names like the Eugenics Education Society and the Race Hygiene Society included university presidents, leading scientists, religious leaders, and other public intellectuals. George Bernard Shaw, Alexander Graham Bell, and Winston Churchill were some of the many luminaries associated with the eugenics movement. It is of course also well known that the German Nazis used a radical version of eugenics to legitimate their vision of a "pure race" of Aryans undiluted by the "inferior" blood of the Jew and other "undesirables."

THE SOCIALLY CONSTRUCTED PERSON

With the advantage of historical perspective it is easy for most of us to recognize "witches" and "missing links" as actual human individuals who had the misfortune of being socially categorized and publicly defined as nonpersons. At the same time, the historical experience of witches and missing links illustrates with frightening clarity that the definition of an individual is "up for grabs." We are not naturally considered fully human; our status as an individual is the consequence of a social process. Where we are born, when we are born, and the relative power of our ancestors can affect how others perceive us. In this sense it is no coincidence that Julia Pastrana, Krao, and Ota Benga were from families and communities that had been either enslaved or economically dominated by European and American colonizers. Nor is it a coincidence that the vast majority of those accused of being demons in the seventeenth century happened to be poor women. Power matters in the classification process. With greater power comes greater authority to establish the criteria for personhood.

The very same social forces of classification are at work today. The categories have certainly changed—witches and missing links are no longer considered legitimate—but the process of creating and using stereotypes is still a fundamental feature of social life. And since the social categorization of others is an essential aspect of social interaction, it is safe to say that this process of *social construction* will always be with us. In the remainder of this chapter we will see how social categories not only structure our perception of others but also serve as the foundation for our thoughts and our emotions. In other words, how we think and what we feel are fundamentally social in nature. To begin to understand the process of social construction we must first examine the nature of language and gain an appreciation for the power of symbols.

LANGUAGE AND THE POWER OF SYMBOLS

When Eunice Cole was accused of being a witch in 1660, the evidence presented at her trial included testimony that she had engaged in "unseemly speeches" by calling Mingay Hussie a "whore" and Mingay's husband a "whore master." In 1673 she was again accused of witchcraft by John Mason, who testified that "Eunice Cole called me devil and said she would split out my brains and the next day I took sick and lay sick about a fortnight after." By today's standards these accusations appear mild, even laughable, but in the context of seventeenth-century New England, they were quite serious. The separation between religion and government did not exist, and the idea of free speech had not yet been developed. Public profanity was often treated as a severe offense, and the words of a witch were thought to be capable of producing physical harm.

Much has changed over the past 350 years, but the power of words has not. Even with a democratic form of governance, the constitutional right to free speech, and the separation of church and state, U.S. citizens can be jailed for the spoken word. That is what happened in 1983 to Larry Flint, the controversial publisher of *Hustler* magazine. The incident occurred while Mr. Flint was representing himself on charges of libel before the Supreme Court of the United States. At one point during the proceedings, Mr. Flint became especially upset and shouted, "Fuck this court!" He then further insulted the nine justices by calling them "nothing but eight assholes and a token cunt." The chief justice responded by ordering Flint's immediate arrest for contempt of court.

In the United States it is also a violation of federal law to utter "any obscene, indecent, or profane language by means of radio communication."[8] This was the issue in the celebrated case of Howard Stern, the so-called radio shock-jock. Stern's show was eventually dropped by Clear Channel Communications after he accumulated fines of nearly $500,000 for the "obscene and profane" words he used on his program.

The power of words is not limited to the world of entertainment or politics. In most every school district in the country, students can be expelled for the use of language that is considered profane, and teachers can be fired for using the same words in the classroom. And of course the power of a word is not limited to the negative reactions of profane use. Consider how much emotion and anxiety can be associated with the word "love" or the expression "I love you."

So why are words so powerful? How can the utterance of a single word produce such strong reactions? And what role does language play in *becoming a person*? The answer to this question begins with an appreciation of *symbols* and *signs*. Words are a special type of symbol, and symbols are a special type of sign. In our everyday language we often use the words "symbol" and "sign" interchangeably. We may say, for example, that a red traffic light is a *symbol* to stop, or that the same light is equivalent to a stop *sign*. Sociologists, however, make an important distinction between symbols and signs. To begin with, signs are less powerful than symbols. Almost all living organisms rely on signs in one form or another, but humans are the only species to create, teach, and use symbols.

Anybody with a dog or cat knows that a pet has an uncanny ability to anticipate the actions of its owner. A dog will begin to salivate and drool at the sight of its food bowl, and it may run to the door and wag its tail if it sees its owner grab a walking leash. Cats have been known to meow with excitement at the sound of an electric can opener, and our own family cat will run and hide under a bed when she senses that we are about to put her outside. In each of these examples, the pet is responding to a sign or series of signs. A sign is in this sense an action or object that comes to represent something else; the can opener is a sign for food, and a leash becomes a sign for a walk to the park. All signs are at some level learned responses. In the natural world, signs become essential to survival. Wild animals learn to navigate their physical environment by responding to signs. Birds learn when to migrate by learning the signs of a new season, deer move deeper into the forest at the first signs of a hunter, and salmon learn to initiate their journey upriver in reaction to water temperature and water depth.

A symbol, in contrast, is a sign that has been intentionally created and has a meaning that is shared by a community of symbol users. Ask yourself, which animals can create and respond to signs they themselves have created? Gorillas? Chimpanzees? Dolphins? Some of these animals appear to learn basic symbol use while under human captivity, but there is little evidence that they can create and modify their own arbitrary signs and share the newly established meaning with others in their species. So far, only humans have demonstrated this unique capacity. This does not mean that other animal species do not communicate. Grunts, barks, growls, chirps, gestures, wing flaps, and so on, are all used to communicate. But these vocalizations and body movements are signs and not symbols. They are limited to the natural world and produce a habitual response that rarely changes.

A symbol, on the other hand, is arbitrary and can be changed rather easily. In American culture, holding up two fingers can mean "peace" or "two." The utterance "yoo" can refer to a letter in the alphabet (u), a pronoun (you), or a type of tree (yew). But a dog's snarl, standing fur, and arched back signals aggression. This "meaning" cannot be *intentionally* changed by other dogs or interpreted any differently. As humans we also use facial expressions and body posture to communicate anger and aggression, but we are not limited to the use of these physical gestures. In certain contexts we can also use words like "whore," "asshole," and "cunt" to represent our aggression. This is what got Eunice Cole and Larry Flint in trouble. Both were arrested for their word choice. Words are symbols that have the power to represent ideas, plans, intentions, and actions. With words we gain the ability to create, organize, reflect, and strategize. This is why words are so powerful. Without the capacity to use symbols, none of these skills would be possible.

Words can be spoken, written, or represented with hand gestures, and when words are combined into a structured system of meaning, we have the basic elements of language. For this reason we can say that nonhuman animals do not create language. Communication through signs is not considered language; language is defined by the use of symbols.[9] When anthropologists in the nineteenth century examined Krao, the so-called ape-girl, they were surprised and impressed that she had mastered several languages. To these naive scientists, it was an amazing feat for a nonhuman. And when Eunice Cole was brought to trial on charges of being a witch, one accuser claimed that she had produced noises that sounded like "the whining of puppies when they have a mind to suck," evidence that Eunice was not fully human.

Humans are born with the potential to communicate symbolically, but this uniquely human capacity will not develop if we are isolated from other humans. Language can only exist in a community of other language users. This is why the quality of early child care is so critical for future development. If we do not interact with other language users, we will not learn to speak or communicate symbolically; and if interaction is limited, our language ability will be stunted. Case studies of children who have been abandoned, neglected, or otherwise separated from human contact support this point. The fictional account of Tarzan would be impossible in real life. A jungle boy who is raised by apes as a child and is skilled at symbolic communication as an adult is a complete fantasy. There is no such thing as a private language. While it is possible to have a *sign* with a unique and private response, *symbols* are by definition public and shared.

As we all know, learning language as a child is a gradual process that initially involves imitation of sounds. Small children can be taught to say words before they understand the symbolic meaning of the word. When my youngest son, Sam, was a preschooler I would ask him to "name three important sociological theorists," and he would proudly proclaim, "Marx, Weber, and Durkheim!" It was a cute trick at the time. Sam obviously had no understanding of the words in the question or the words in his response. For Sam, the words were signs and not symbols. I also remember a similar incident with my son Patrick. One afternoon when Patrick was about three years old, we wandered into a pet shop that had a large parrot perched prominently in the center of the store. It was a beautiful and noisy bird that had been taught to mimic three expressions "Hello," "What's your name?" and "My name is Polly." Patrick made a beeline to the bird's cage and stood there, staring up at the talking parrot. When the parrot squawked "Hello," Patrick responded timidly with a soft "Hi." But when the bird mimicked "What's your name?" my young son gleefully replied, "Patrick! What's your name?" At this exact moment, the bird randomly produced its third phrase, "My name is Polly." Well, needless to say, Patrick was convinced that he had discovered a real talking bird, and he quickly launched into a long story about his family, toys, and friends, oblivious to the fact that Polly was still repeating the same three phrases.

As we grow and mature from an infant to an adult, our capacity to learn, use, and create symbols is nurtured within a language community. This process is common to all people in all societies, and it begins with learning signs. Thus, we first learn to mimic sounds and associate sounds with objects and people. A baby learns to say "Mama" or "Dada" with repeated coaching from his or her parents. The word "hot" is associated with the oven, or the word "bye" is linked to leaving the house. At this rudimentary stage of language use, the words "Mama," "hot," and "bye" are symbols in an adult's vocabulary, but they remain only signs for the child. The child's use of these words is still quite limited, and so this form of communication is more similar to a parrot and a dog than it is to an adult human. The process of turning signs into symbols occurs over time within a community of language users who sustain the necessary conditions. By way of analogy, think of a pinecone that falls onto an asphalt parking lot; under these stark environmental conditions it will never become a tree. But the same pinecone that lands on a moist forest floor, with sufficient sun and rain, could eventually become a magnificent lodge pole pine. In the same way, we are born with the biological capacity to become powerful language users, but without the right social environment, this defining feature of our personhood will lie dormant and remain unrealized.

The difference between communication based on signs and communication based on symbols cannot be overemphasized. The leap from *sign responder* to *symbol user* has immense sociological consequences. With the use of symbols we can create great works of art, magnificent architectural structures, and complex institutions of education, law, and religion. Symbols are also the foundation for reading, writing, science, and philosophy. On the darker side, symbols make war, torture, and genocide possible, as well as personal humiliation, discrimination, and exploitation. A single symbol can evoke all of these emotions and spark a range of intense social action.

The power of symbols is plainly evident at the University of Mississippi, where a flag and the school mascot have provoked raucous debate, public demonstrations, lawsuits, and acts of collective defiance for more than a decade. On one side of the controversy are those who want to preserve a "cultural heritage" represented by the Confederate battle flag and a cartoon mascot known as "Colonel Reb." For these "traditionalists," the symbols represent southern pride and a history of solidarity and defiance during the Civil War. The flag is said to honor the thousands of rebel soldiers who gave their lives in defense of the old South, and the soldier mascot is said to symbolize school spirit and a heritage of athletic success. On the other side of the debate are those who view the rebel flag and rebel soldier as representations of a racist heritage and a time when slavery and segregation prevailed. For this group, the symbols evoke powerful images of violence, lynchings, and a time on campus in the 1960s when federal marshals and the National Guard were used to enforce civil rights legislation and protect the life of James Meredith, the first black student to enroll at "Ole Miss." Moreover, to the opponents of the flag and mascot, the vociferous support for these symbols is evidence that a culture of racism is still very much alive in Mississippi and on the University of Mississippi campus. As recently as 2007, Robert Khayat, the top university administrator who banned the mascot and discouraged displays of the rebel flag, received periodic death threats and required a bodyguard for protection.

Clearly, symbols such as words, a flag, a cartoon character, a cross, or an extended middle finger produce more than a simple conditioned response. The deeply meaningful reactions they generate cannot be explained in terms of habit or instinct. This is because symbols and symbolic interaction are at the very core of our thinking, our emotions, and our identity as individuals.

THE SOCIOLOGY OF THOUGHT

Most people assume that *thinking* is something that goes on inside our heads. Most of us believe that our thoughts are private, personal, subjective, and secret. To some extent this is true. It is possible to keep our reasoning, our beliefs, and our judgments hidden from others. Nevertheless, the way we think, the way we learn to think, the categories we think with, and the topics we think about all begin on the outside, in the social world, and depend on shared symbols, language, and community. In this way, our thinking is public *before* it is private, and for the same reason, personal thoughts are never quite real until they are exposed to the reaction of others and tested for truth and legitimacy in symbolic communication. Bridget Bishop fiercely defended her personal belief that she was not a witch, and Julia Pastrana never doubted her private commitment to being fully human, but neither woman could overcome the dominant public understandings that determined their ultimate fate.

When sociologists talk about thinking, or *social cognition*, they are actually referring to a number of different but related processes—how we pay attention, the categories we use to classify things in the world, the meaning things have for us, and our ability to remember and process information. All of these mental activities depend on using symbols and involve imagination, the anticipation of a future, and an assessment of the past. Animals and infants do not possess these skills and therefore are not capable of social cognition. Animals and infants certainly have brain activity, and they are able to process information in their environment, but without symbols they cannot hold the world in their heads. They cannot re-create the past or fantasize about a future. They cannot stare for hours on end at sheets of paper covered with black markings and experience the curiosity, intrigue, terror, joy, and sadness that come with reading. In other words, without symbols, letters and sentences have no meaning; without symbols, the world is only experienced in the here and now; and without symbols, the creative manipulation and testing of new ideas cannot occur.

At one level, social cognition is quite literally a conversation with one's self. When we are engaged in reflective thought we are taking symbolic communication and holding it inside our heads. We are not born with this sophisticated form of thinking; it is something that develops along with the ability to convert signs into symbols. We become better at it by exercising our imaginative powers, which is why fantasy and role-playing are critical for child development. My daughter Emilia was typical of many children when, at age two, she would actively engage in conversations with imaginary characters. For most children, fantasy role-playing is not limited to representations of real people who happen to be absent from the scene. Rather, they tend to be completely fictional characters and may even be animals. In Emilia's case, she held lengthy and complex conversations with an entire family of pigs—even though we lived in the city and her only contact with swine was through picture books, television, and movies. When toddlers engage in such behavior we tend to see it as endearing and cute. We recognize it for what it is—a stage in the development of language and thought. However, with age and increasing socialization, we expect these overt instances of role-playing to disappear. If my daughter were to renew her acquaintance with the pig family at the age of twenty-five, there would be reason for concern. In an earlier era, she might be required to undergo a physical examination for the markings of a witch. Today, if she were consistently engaged in out-loud conversations with her imaginary barnyard buddies, we would no doubt suggest a psychological examination.

As we grow older, our role-playing fantasies are usually internalized and covert and our imaginations are hidden from public view. While a child can get away with immediately verbalizing every thought and every question that pops up, adults must learn to control their opinions, harness impulses, and stifle reactions. This is especially true in situations where one is relatively powerless. The boss, for example, can evaluate you, critique your performance, and dictate everything from the clothes you wear to the hours you work, but if you want to keep your job, you must keep your thoughts about your boss to yourself, or at least out of earshot.

Imaginary role-playing is an exercise in learning how to engage in what sociologists call *role-taking*. Role-taking is the ability to see the world from someone else's perspective. It is similar to empathy and sympathy, and it requires getting imaginarily into someone else's head, anticipating their reactions, and adjusting one's own actions accordingly. When a mother with a newborn makes plans for a long trip, she will take the role of her baby and anticipate his feeding and sleeping schedule and adjust her itinerary accordingly. Her baby, on the other hand, will not adjust his demand for food or adopt a more flexible feeding routine so as to make life easier for Mom. Is the baby selfish, self-centered, and uncaring? Perhaps, but not in the way we would normally use these terms. The baby is incapable of taking the role of others and as a consequence has no power to accommodate others' needs or expectations.

With more complex language skills we also develop more sophisticated role-taking skills. We learn to take the role of more than one person at the same time, something that comes in handy in the more complicated interactions of everyday adulthood. Anyone who has ever tried to teach a group of preschoolers how to play a game of basketball, soccer, or baseball can appreciate the frustrations that result from not being able to engage in simultaneous role-taking. These young children usually have very rudimentary language skills and therefore have difficulty understanding the rules of a game from multiple perspectives. Because their use of symbols is still very basic, preschoolers cannot comprehend the idea of different positions with different roles that are all relevant to one's immediate action. For this reason, very young basketball players all want to dribble and shoot but not pass, set a screen, or cut to the hoop. Soccer players all swarm around the ball in an attempt to kick a goal, and baseball players will wander off the field unless they are hitting or catching. No amount of coaching, diagramming, screaming, bribing, or modeling is going to succeed if a certain level of symbol use has not been reached. Waiting, anticipating, and coordinating action with your teammates requires a level of social maturity that comes with using symbols in a sophisticated manner.

George Herbert Mead (1863–1931), one of the founders of American sociology, called this skill "taking the role of the generalized other," and it is as relevant and necessary in everyday life as it is in playing a sport. When we act, we must take account of how others in the immediate situation will respond, and we must consider how it will be viewed by others who may not be present—our family, our friends, a teacher, a boss, the police, and so forth. In addition to specific others, we may also take into account the position of "the church," "the audience," or a sense of "what is cool" or might be "lame." It is in this generalized way that society gets into our heads.

GROUP DIFFERENCES IN SOCIAL COGNITION

The ability to learn symbols, employ role-taking skills, and engage in reflective conversation with one's self is a style of thinking common to our species. This proficiency with symbols is shared by all biologically healthy adults who have been adequately socialized. This does not mean, however, that we all think in the same way. Psychologists have shown that there are *individual* differences in how new information is learned, mentally organized, processed, and remembered. Some people, for example, may learn better with visual information, while others do better with information that they hear. For sociologists, these personal differences are interesting but of marginal relevance since they tell us little about our connection to society. What is of particular importance from a sociological point of view is how thinking patterns reflect different *thought communities*. Research has demonstrated that there are significant differences among social groups in terms of how we think. Some of these distinctions reflect cultural differences, some are historical, some are based on social class or ethnicity, and all are grounded in the fact that different groups have different social experiences.[10]

For example, when Americans are asked to look at a photograph or short video of a fish tank, they tend to focus almost exclusively on the fish while ignoring the "background" items like rocks, plants, and bubbles. But when Japanese and Chinese subjects are asked to examine the same image, they do not immediately zoom in on the fish. Instead, they are more likely to pay attention to the entire tank and see the fish as part of a larger interconnected environment. This difference in "perception" or "attention" also seems to affect memory. Americans remember the fish with some detail but don't do as well in recalling the other items in the tank. East Asians, on the other hand, have much better memory of the whole tank. Similar studies using different images and different cultural comparisons produce the same findings. How do we account for such differences in perception and memory? In this case, it likely reflects the fact that East Asian cultures tend to place less emphasis on individualism and as a result tend to "think" more holistically, with greater attention to relationships and connections among people and things. Because American culture stresses independence and autonomy, Americans are more likely to notice discrete objects as separate from the larger context.[11]

Some cultural differences in our habits of thinking may be trivial, while others may have important sociological consequences. Consider, for example, the difference between Chinese and American interpretations of deviant behavior. When American newspaper reporters attempt to explain why a murder has occurred, they tend to focus on the personal characteristics and limitations of the individual who committed the act. To most Americans this seems like an obvious approach to interpreting bad behavior. However, Chinese-language newspapers covering the same crime in the United States tend to take a very different approach. Instead of focusing on the qualities of the murderer, they are much more likely to consider the *situational* factors that may have contributed to the crime—loss of a job, death of a friend, and so on.

This difference in what is called the *attribution of responsibility* is additional evidence that cultural experiences and traditions are sometimes reflected in different styles of perception and interpretation of the social world. American individualism contributes to a much stronger emphasis on personal responsibility while Chinese culture contributes to a more *collectivist* orientation. [12]

It is very important to stress that group differences in social cognition are *not* the result of genetic or other physiological differences. This is a critical point of emphasis. In the past, eugenicists and other racist and sexist organizations used the developing authority and prestige of science to argue that groups differed in terms of "inherited intelligence." Skulls and brains were photographed, measured, and weighed in a determined effort to show that Africans, Asians, Native Americans, and women were intellectually inferior to white, Anglo-Saxon, Protestant (WASP) males. The findings were then used to explain why criminal behavior and poor educational achievement was more likely to be found with some groups. It was also used to justify wide-ranging group discrimination that kept women and ethnic minorities from achieving important civil rights, like the right to vote. We now know that this research was scientifically flawed and biased in favor of the scientists who conducted the research. It is no coincidence that the evidence that supposedly showed WASP males to be the most intelligent group of people was collected and analyzed by WASP males using their own preferred definition of intelligence. [13]

Along these same lines it is also important to emphasize that the mere fact that groups differ in terms of social cognition does *not* mean that one style is inherently superior to another. Our shared experience with different physical and social environments leads to group variation. Whether one style is "better" than another depends upon who is making the judgment and how much power is in the hands of the judgment maker. When the first IQ (intelligence quotient) tests were developed by psychologists in the early 1900s, they included questions that equated intelligence with American middle-class education and lifestyle. For example, the IQ test used by the army in 1923 contained the following items:

1. The forward pass is used in . . . tennis, hockey, football, golf?
2. The Brooklyn Nationals are called the . . . Giants, Orioles, Superbas, Indians?

3. The Pierce Arrow car is made in . . . Buffalo, Detroit, Toledo, Flint?

4. "There's a Reason" is an ad for a . . . drink, revolver, flour, cleanser?

It should be obvious from reading these questions that immigrants from another country, those uninterested in American sports, or those unfamiliar with American consumer culture would not score high on this measure of IQ. But tests such as these were assumed to be impartial and unbiased. They were used by officials at Ellis Island to prevent "defective" immigrants from entering the United States, and IQ evidence was used to specifically limit the influx of Jews, Italians, Slavs, Japanese, and Chinese. Even more severely, the results from similar IQ tests were used to justify the forced sterilization of men and women deemed "unfit for propagation." In a typical law passed by the Virginia legislature in 1924, inmates of state institutions could be legally sterilized if "the said inmate is insane, idiotic, imbecile, feeble-minded, or epileptic." It is estimated that some sixty thousand forced sterilizations occurred in the United States between 1907 and 1968 as part of a strategy to limit the reproduction of citizens who did not think or act in a socially desirable manner. [14]

The forced sterilization of "imbeciles," the enslavement of "missing links," and the hanging of "witches" represent different historical reactions to individuals who were classified as deviant by the cultural, political, scientific, and religious authorities of the day. By today's standards, these cases appear bizarre. But dominant social categories and styles of cognition helped to "normalize" and legitimate the abuse. These cruelties were perceived by many as not only acceptable but also righteous. It is hard to believe that devout Christians of Europe could gather in a public square, view someone being burned alive at the stake, and walk away with a sense of satisfaction and justice. Were these people emotionless and devoid of feeling? Of course not. The fact that we can react with horror, disgust, and anger at these historical atrocities demonstrates that social cognition has an emotional component and that our emotions are not independent of social forces.

THE SOCIOLOGY OF EMOTION

In a famous series of experiments conducted in the early 1960s, researchers used an ingenious but highly controversial technique to investigate the social foundation of emotions.[15] Subjects in the experiments were led to believe that they were participating in a study about the effects of a "vitamin injection." In truth, the injection they received was a small dose of epinephrine (adrenaline), a drug that stimulates the nervous system and produces a degree of physiological arousal. Half the subjects in one condition of the experiment were told that the "vitamins" would lead to an increased heart rate, flushed face, and slight trembling; while in another condition the other half of the volunteers were given no information at all about side effects. The researchers speculated that the subjects who had no explanation for their arousal would be more susceptible to having their emotions manipulated. This, in fact, is what they discovered. When placed in a room with an exuberantly happy person, the subjects with no explanation of the drug's effects reported that they were also feeling euphoric and positive. When placed in a room with an angry person, the uninformed subjects reported feeling hostile and negative. But if subjects knew that their arousal was the result of the injection, their mood was largely unaffected by the reactions of those around them.

This experiment is significant in that it was one of the first studies to demonstrate that emotions are dependent upon a social label. When we experience physiological arousal, the explanation we give to our feelings will be influenced by the reactions of others, our expectations of what our mood should be, and the cultural labels we use to name our feelings. In this way, emotions are socially constructed. When we experience anger, joy, fear, or sadness, our body responds in very noticeable ways, but society provides the vocabulary for making sense of these sensations. Without language, our sentiments would not be as diverse and complex. The feelings experienced by an infant are basic and unsophisticated. Babies don't experience revenge, lust, jealousy, disgust, shame, or guilt. These advanced sentiments develop over time and within a community of symbol users.

Community is also where we learn to "control" our emotions and respond in an "appropriate" manner according to specific *feeling rules*. Because we experience emotions in a very personal way, it is sometimes difficult to recognize that our feelings are also structured by social expectations. In fact, every social setting has associated with it an emotional script that indicates the appropriate mood of the various actors. The feeling rules associated with a funeral, a wedding, a party, the birth of a baby, or a graduation ceremony are rather obvious, but there are also more subtle feeling rules that apply to specific encounters and particular roles.

Consider, for example, the emotionally delicate relationship between a physician and a patient when a physical examination of the genitals or other "private part" is required. The doctor must maintain a professional, nonchalant demeanor while at the same time demonstrating feelings of respect and care. The patient, on the other hand, is expected to remain composed and cooperative, while avoiding displays of fear, anxiety, or embarrassment. In such an encounter, emotions associated with laughter, romance, shock, or joy are deliberately avoided. This is not an easy task. The participants must learn both the appropriate feelings and how to maintain the feelings in what would normally be a very uncomfortable, even disturbing procedure. Physicians usually have the advantage of experience and training as they begin to learn different techniques for managing their feelings while in medical school. This includes using medically appropriate technical language and learning how to depersonalize and objectify the patient. This can be seen in the following quotes taken from a study of emotion management in medical school. [16]

> When we were dissecting the pelvis, the wrong words kept coming to mind, and it was uncomfortable. I tried to be sure to use the right words, penis and testicles (pause) not cock and balls.
> —First-year female student

> You can't tell what's wrong without looking under the hood. It's different when I'm talking with a patient. But when I'm examining them it's like an automobile engine. . . . There's a bad connotation with that, but it's literally what I mean.
> —Third-year male student

In this example, we can see that the medical school and other health-care institutions are important locations for learning both the physical and emotional aspects of practicing medicine.

In the modern world, institutions play an increasing role in the control and management of emotions. This is particularly evident in the workplace, where many industries are in the businesses of selling an emotional state. Disneyland advertises its theme parks as "the happiest place on Earth"; Las Vegas casinos promote risk and eroticism with the assurance that "what happens in Vegas, stays in Vegas"; the Hollywood movie industry depends on its films to produce a range of emotions that leave us feeling "entertained"; and everything from cars to sneakers is now sold using ad campaigns that promise emotional renewal. Phil Knight, cofounder of Nike, Inc., was one of the first to capitalize on the selling of emotion even though he was in the business of producing athletic shoes. As he described it, "We're not in the fashion business, as the *Wall Street Journal* wrote the other day. We're in the sports business, and there's a big difference. . . . Sports is like rock 'n roll. Both are dominant cultural forces, both speak an international language, and both are all about emotions."

When a company is selling emotions, it expects its employees to contribute to the mood-altering experience. Disneyland employees should be happy, Las Vegas casino hostesses should be sexy and flirtatious, and Nike representatives should be energetic and athletically fit. More important still, these employers require their employees to be *genuinely* happy, flirtatious, and energetic. Fake feeling from stiff and robotic employees is unacceptable to corporate supervisors. This is why Wal-Mart hires kind and elderly greeters, why Starbucks hires trendy and hip baristas, and why Hooters hires young and perky waitresses. But when feeling rules become employment rules, it is not easy to be sincere. No one is capable of always feeling happy, sexy, kind, or energetic, especially while working forty to fifty hours a week for a demanding company and equally demanding customers.

While traditional manufacturing jobs, construction work, and truck driving may be "back breaking" and physically challenging, the newer service industry jobs are "emotionally draining." When working on an assembly line, picking vegetables, or roofing a house, one does not have regular face-to-face engagement with a customer, and so there are few who expect you to maintain a sincere smile, engaging personality, or sunny disposition. But counselors, sales clerks, tour guides, and other service-sector employees all struggle to produce expected emotions for their employers while working jobs that can be boring, frustrating, or offensive. Despite the expectations of the company, one's emotions cannot be turned on and off with a switch. Tears and anxiety from one's home life can leak into one's work life, and personal crises with family or friends cannot always be contained in personal places. For this reason, working a job that requires "emotional labor" can have greater psychological risks than a job that requires "physical labor."

This is what sociologist Arlie Hochschild discovered in her study of airline flight attendants. [17] She found that veteran flight attendants who worked for years according to the company "feeling rules" often struggled with depression, periods of "emotional deadness," and a confused sense of true identity. Forcing oneself to "act" in a genuinely positive manner by ignoring or burying other emotions is, it turns out, psychologically unhealthy. Moreover, according to Hochschild, the issues associated with emotion management tend to be more prevalent among the poor and among women. With fewer resources to control one's life, poor women are less able to defend against the emotional demands of others.

Not surprisingly, related research has shown that the commercialization of human feeling and the loss of emotional control in the workplace are associated with a growing cultural concern with authenticity and a preoccupation with "finding one's true self." Cultural indicators of this abound. For example, in 2012, the *New York Times* list of bestselling books included advice on how to lose weight, how to improve one's marriage, how to make more money, how to look younger, and how to "get what you want" from others. Titles such as *Change Your Words, Change Your Life*, *How to Lose Weight without Dieting or Working Out*, and *The Seven Habits of Highly Effective People: Powerful Lessons in Personal Change* promise strategies for reshaping the self while offering a path toward a more fulfilling and emotionally satisfying life. In a similar manner, the popularity of television and radio talk show hosts like Oprah, Dr. Phil, and Dr. Laura demonstrate that there is a large American audience searching for emotional connection and in need of direction and certainty.

When books don't do the trick, Americans have demonstrated an increasing fascination with risky behavior—what sociologists call *edgework*. Edgework refers to the practice of voluntarily engaging in behavior that has a very high risk of producing physical harm and borders on the margin between life and death. It includes dangerous sports such as mountain climbing, parachuting, hang gliding, and whitewater rafting, as well as criminal acts such as carjacking, car racing, and experimenting with drugs. Because it is risky, edgework produces a level of excitement and an emotional "rush" that is largely absent from the stultifying, routine, and boring life of many modern bureaucracies. Edgework is in this sense a form of escape and resistance that allows for intense feelings and a degree of self-determination and control that is not found at work, school, or home. [18]

THE SOCIOLOGY OF IDENTITY

We began this chapter with a brief historical review of two very different types of identities—witches and missing links. In the seventeenth century, witches were causing fear and panic across Europe and New England, and in the latter part of the nineteenth century, missing links created a similar stir throughout the very same region. Today, however, the witches have disappeared and the missing links are once again missing. So what happened? Did the devil stop sending his handmaidens? Did the missing links go extinct?

With the advantage of historical and sociological perspective, we can now easily recognize that witches and missing links were in fact social inventions. Over time, as religious fundamentalism declined, community members stopped searching for witches, and as racist interpretations of evolution were discredited, the public no longer expected to find missing links. Like all social constructions, these two historically powerful social identities required hungry hearts and searching minds to maintain their public existence. In much the same way that an ancient language dies out when no one is around to speak it, social identities can also disappear if they are not actively deployed in a community. In modern society witches no longer evoke and maintain the same emotional fervor, and missing links are unable to generate and sustain the same intellectual interest. As a consequence both social identities have vanished from the cultural landscape.

While it may be easy for us to appreciate the fact that witches and missing links were socially constructed, it is more difficult to accept the fact that *all* of our social identities are in a similar manner socially constructed. This means that any label or category we use to identify one another can potentially disappear or become obsolete and therefore become "not real." This includes identities associated with our occupations (e.g., telegraph operator, swordsmith); our religious beliefs (e.g., exorcist, mumifier); our leisure activities (buggy rider, snuff taking); and even identities that appear to be natural, such as those that identify us in terms of family (mother, brother, cousin), gender (male, female), or race (black, white), which are in fact social constructions. We know from research that has examined social identities in different cultures and in different historical periods that there are very few categories that are common to all people in all times. For example, in Yorubaland of West Africa (present-day Nigeria), the concept of woman did not exist as a relevant social category prior to contact with Western colonizers. [19]

And in the United States, the Irish immigrants of the late 1800s were not initially considered to be "white" by the Europeans who had already established a dominant position of power in America.[20] The evidence is unequivocal: the existence of an identity category and the boundaries of an identity category are not permanent.

It is at least theoretically possible, therefore, that at some point in the future there will be no racial or gender categories that are noticed and used as a social classification scheme. This, however, would require a level of social and economic equality that we do not presently experience. Racial categories were originally invented by powerful people to justify and legitimate slavery, oppression, and segregation, and until the damage that they have created has been overcome, race will continue to be a powerful social construction. The same is true of gender-based distinctions as well. While the categories of male and female will undoubtedly remain biologically pertinent, their social and personal significance could conceivably fade to the point of irrelevance.

At one level, social identities are just words, but as we saw earlier in this chapter, words are also symbols and symbols have powerful social consequences. Symbols structure the way we think, are deeply connected to our emotions, and are the basis of our social interaction. In the case of race and gender identities, they also have considerable political and economic consequences. To end race or gender-based discrimination, it is not enough to simply say we should stop employing labels or avoid making generalizations. This is a naive individualist response to a complex sociological phenomenon. Social identities will always structure our actions and will always be used at some level to identify and distinguish each of us from one another. We can, however, work to extinguish harmful social classification schemes and alter the more destructive meanings associated with some of our social identities. But to do so, we must first recognize that inequality is socially produced in social interactions that are structured by powerful social forces.

Chapter Three

Conformity and Disobedience

The Power of the Group

Authority exercised with humility and obedience accepted with delight are the very lines along which our spirits live.

—C. S. Lewis [1]

Strengthen the female mind by enlarging it, and there will be an end to blind obedience.

—Mary Wollstonecraft [2]

It was five o'clock on a Friday afternoon and the dinner rush was just getting underway at the McDonald's restaurant in Mount Washington, Kentucky. Louise Ogburn, a senior at Spencer County High School, was working the counter while her supervisor, fifty-one-year-old Donna Summers, was taking care of paperwork in the back office. By all accounts Louise was a model citizen and an eager worker with a squeaky clean employment record. For this reason, Donna was surprised when the company phone rang and an "Officer Scott" said that an employee matching Louise Ogburn's description was being investigated for stealing a customer's purse. The police officer on the other end of the line said that he was in contact with both the senior store manager and a representative from McDonald's corporate headquarters. Donna was then instructed to bring Louise into the office for an interrogation and to hold her there until police arrived. In the meantime, Donna was told to remain on the phone and carefully follow the officer's instructions. A surveillance camera located in the manager's office recorded the astonishing sequence of events that followed.[3]

Louise was stunned. She denied stealing anything from anybody. The videotape showed Louise trembling and in tears. It also showed Donna on the phone, following detailed instructions from Officer Scott. Louise was first asked to empty her pockets of all belongings, including car keys, cell phone, and identification. Then, surprisingly, Donna was told to conduct a strip search of her young employee to ensure that she wasn't hiding any items under her McDonald's uniform. Donna did not hesitate and ordered Louise to remove all of her clothing, including her underwear. Louise would later say that she did as she was told "because they were a higher authority to me" and "I was scared for my own safety because I thought I was in trouble with the law." But Louise's bizarre ordeal had just begun; she would continue to undergo the "interrogation" for another two and a half hours as the phone instructions from Officer Scott grew more extreme.

When Donna had to leave the office to perform her duties as assistant manager, Officer Scott demanded that she find another employee to monitor Louise. Donna turned to Jason Scott (no relation to Officer Scott), a twenty-seven-year-old cook, who entered the cramped office and found Louise in shock, attempting to cover herself with a small apron. Still on the phone, Officer Scott told Jason to take the apron away from Louise; Jason refused and returned to the kitchen, disgusted by the spectacle. Nevertheless, neither Jason nor another assistant manager who saw Louise naked in the office made any attempt to intervene. Louise wanted to make a run for it, but without her clothes she said she was too humiliated to risk being seen in public.

With no one available to serve as a guard, Officer Scott now asked Donna if her husband could come in to assist with the surveillance. Donna informed the officer that she was not married but that her fiancé, Walter Nix, might be available. When Walter showed up around 6:00 p.m., he too proved to be an obedient and compliant assistant, and like Donna, he dutifully followed the telephoned directives. Only now, the instructions were even more incredibly disturbing.

For more than an hour, Nix followed orders that required a naked Louise Ogburn to jump up and down and stand on a chair to see if any drugs would "shake out." At one point when Louise refused to obey, Nix was told to spank the petrified teenager—which he did, repeatedly for several minutes. Then in an unbelievable act of aggression, Louise was ordered onto her knees, and forced to perform oral sex on Mr. Nix.

When she protested and begged for mercy, Nix threatened to beat her—all while maintaining the phone conversation with Officer Scott.

Louise Ogburn's nightmare ended when Thomas Simms was asked by Donna to relieve Walter Nix and continue the interrogation. However, Mr. Simms, a fifty-eight-year-old maintenance man who worked at the restaurant, refused Officer Scott's perverse demands and told Donna Summers that something was seriously wrong. A panicked Donna Summers called her supervisor, whom she believed was on another line with Officer Scott. It was then that she learned that the entire ordeal had been a vicious hoax perpetrated by an anonymous caller posing as Officer Scott. Neither the local police department nor McDonald's corporate leaders were linked to the phone call.

Soon after the scam, McDonald's fired Donna Summers. She was eventually sentenced to probation after being charged with unlawful imprisonment. Mr. Nix pleaded guilty to sexual abuse and unlawful imprisonment and received a five-year sentence. Both Ms. Summers and Mr. Nix strongly defended their belief that they were following the orders of a legitimate police detective. A subsequent police investigation failed to convict the perpetrator of the hoax.

Louise Ogburn was seriously traumatized by the event. According to court depositions, she suffers from panic attacks, depression, and nightmares. In 2007, a jury found the fast-food giant guilty of negligence and ordered the company to pay Louise $6.1 million for medical bills, compensation for pain and suffering, and punitive damages. Donna Summers and Walter Nix broke off their engagement.

If not for the fact that events had been recorded by a security camera, the entire story might be dismissed as an "urban legend" or sick pornographic fiction. Even still, it is tempting to explain the incident from an individualistic perspective as the abnormal behavior of several weak and mentally suspect adults. There is, however, a critical sociological interpretation of this tragic story.

To begin with, the episode is not an isolated incident. It was in fact part of a pattern of similar cruel hoaxes that occurred across the country between 1995 and 2004.

Many of the phone calls were recognized as fraudulent and were ignored. But according to police reports and press accounts, phone calls to at least seventy fast-food restaurants in more than thirty states resulted in an employee or customer stripping naked—or worse. A Burger King manager in Fargo, North Dakota, spanked a teenage employee on her naked buttocks. A McDonald's employee in Leitchfield, Kentucky, stripped in front of a customer. Another McDonald's employee in Roosevelt, Iowa, jogged naked and assumed various embarrassing poses. An Applebee's manager in Davenport, Iowa, conducted a "degrading ninety-minute search of an employee." In Juneau, Alaska, the manager of a Taco Bell stripped a fourteen-year-old customer and forced her to "perform lewd acts." In all of these incidents, the restaurant employees insisted they were simply following orders.

OBEDIENCE TO AUTHORITY

Why would so many people obey orders that are so obviously beyond the bounds of socially acceptable behavior? While this is a critical question, it is not a new problem. Good, ethical citizens have been following bad, unethical instructions from persons of authority for quite some time. It is a dilemma with a long history, and social scientists have been examining this issue in earnest since the end of World War II. When the horror of the Holocaust and other wartime atrocities was revealed, the extent of the brutality shocked and disgusted much of the world. However, like the fast-food restaurant employees, most of the perpetrators of torture and genocide were otherwise "good people" who claimed to be following orders.

It was within this historical context that Professor Stanley Milgram of Yale University (1933–1984) set out to test the social conditions under which an extreme order would be followed. In the early 1960s, he designed a series of related experiments where volunteers were asked to administer a range of electrical shocks to another person under various predetermined situations. The research findings proved to be startling. In the basic design of the experiment, male volunteers from the community were offered a small fee for what they believed would be a study of "the effects of punishment on learning." When the participants arrived at the laboratory, they were greeted by the experimenter dressed in a lab coat and an actor who posed as another volunteer. The participants were then told that through a random draw one of them would serve as the "teacher" and the other would serve as the "learner." In truth, however, the actor was always selected to be the learner. The learner was then strapped to a chair with wire electrodes attached to his wrist. In an adjacent room the teacher was given the controls of an electric generator and was told that his job was to administer an electric shock when instructed by the experimenter. This occurred whenever the learner gave the wrong answer to a long list of memory questions. In addition, the teacher was expected to increase the voltage of the shock each time the learner gave a wrong answer. To make the ordeal even more threatening, the voltage levels on the generator were identified with sequential labels: "slight shock," "strong shock," "danger: severe shock," and finally "XXX."

The volunteer teacher did not know that the electric generator was a fake and that the learner, who could be heard over a speaker, was actually an actor engaged in a performance. With each missed answer and subsequent "shock," the actor/learner reacted with an increasing degree of pain and verbal protest. What began as a slight grunt would eventually evolve into an agonized scream and painful pleading to be released from the chair. At the two highest levels of shock, the actor fell silent, apparently unconscious.

Of the forty male volunteers who participated in the initial experiment, twenty-six followed the experimenter's orders and continued to administer the "shocks" all the way to the maximum XXX level! Interviews conducted after the experiment confirmed that the "teachers" believed they were inflicting serious harm on the "learners." Although most volunteers were uncomfortable proceeding and all showed a degree of concern for their victims, they followed the pain-inflicting instructions and obeyed the directives of a relative stranger despite the fact that the experimenter's only commands were "You must continue" and "You have no other choice; you must go on."

Several follow-up studies by Milgram and others conducted over the past forty years have confirmed a 65 percent rate of compliance to be consistent across various groups of people.[4] Thus, researchers have found that women and citizens of other countries have similarly high rates of obedience under the same experimental conditions. There are, however, certain factors that appear to enhance or deter the likelihood of obedience. Personal, face-to-face contact, for example, seems to be an important factor. When the teacher and learner are placed in the same room or are seated next to each other, the rate of obedience significantly declines. Similarly, when the experimenter gives orders over a telephone or is absent from the room, the orders are less likely to be followed by the teacher. But even when both of these conditions are combined, there is still a significant percentage of people who will continue to comply. Indeed, this is precisely what we saw with the fast-food restaurant hoax. Extreme orders were delivered over the phone and the perpetrator had personal contact with the victims of the abuse. Nevertheless, humiliating and degrading acts were still committed.

The Milgram experiments, the fast-food restaurant hoaxes, and the atrocities of World War II demonstrate the force of group membership. Groups vary in size and influence and can range from a simple two-person work crew to a complex multinational corporation. Some groups, such as a college sorority, may have a relatively long history of volunteer member commitment, while others, such as a court-selected jury, may be short lived and involuntary. We cannot escape group membership—nor should we. Groups provide the fertile social context from which language sprouts. Groups provide security and build trust. Groups anchor our sense of self and provide us with social identities. Our family, work, friendships, play, religion, education, and politics are all experienced in and through group affiliations.

To understand the power of a group is to understand social behavior—both good and bad. Consider the Missionaries of Charity, a religious order of Catholic nuns founded by Mother Teresa (1910–1997). Members of this group make a solemn profession to provide "wholehearted and free service to the poorest of the poor." The sisters also take a lifetime vow of chastity, poverty, and obedience to their group. This is not done lightly. To profess one's identity as a Catholic nun and to adorn oneself with a religious habit is a proclamation of spiritual conviction. It requires an immense intellectual and emotional dedication to the larger group goals.

In much the same way, the members of the Ku Klux Klan (KKK) also profess to uphold and obey the values of their fraternal organization. Like the Missionaries of Charity, the KKK is also founded on religious principles. Members of the Klan pledge to "preserve the Unites States as a Protestant Christian Nation," "to protect . . . the chastity of womanhood," "to inculcate a pure patriotism," and "to maintain the principles of white supremacy." In addition, the brothers of the KKK swear to uphold the values of secrecy, fidelity, and obedience to the brotherhood.[5] To claim affiliation with the KKK and to wear the white, hooded robe is to make a powerful personal and public statement. One does not become a Klansman unless there is at some level an intellectual and emotional commitment to the group ideals.

While no one would ever confuse a Klansman for a nun, there is a similarity in the way the two groups influence and affect their members. To begin with, membership is defined as a privilege that is restricted to a select few. Group leaders must review and evaluate the applicant to determine if he or she is sufficiently committed to the group goals. In this way, acceptance into the group is experienced as an elevation in status and as an honor for which the new member is grateful and appreciative. This is celebrated with a ritual ceremony where a prayer and a formal pledge of allegiance are recited in the presence of the other group members.

In addition, both groups are organized hierarchically with clearly specified roles and obligations. Some members are given more power than others and can expect to have their orders obeyed. Thus, the official structure of the KKK recognizes the "Grand Wizard" as the national leader. In the case of the Missionaries of Charity, Mother Teresa held the post of "Superior General."

When the power structure of a group is accepted as legitimate, it is called "authority." Very often, authority is associated with visible markers such as distinct clothing, patches on a uniform, or a special seat at group meetings. These accoutrements become symbols of power and indicators that deference and respect are in order. In such groups, obedience to authority is not simply something one is required to do; it is something members want to do. When membership is voluntary, desirable, and a significant part of one's social identity, following the directives of a group leader is less likely questioned. It is experienced as the fulfillment of one's obligation, as doing the right thing.

Sometimes when committed group members obey the orders of a leader, it may seem extreme or irrational from the perspective of outsiders. But to insiders, it is understandable and normal. Consider, for example, the McDonald's hoax. Although Donna Summers was not acting as a nun or a member of the KKK, she was a relatively committed member of the McDonald's corporation. In her role as assistant manager she was recognized as having legitimate power—authority— over the other workers at the restaurant. Louise Ogburn recognized and accepted Donna's right to give orders. As a teenager, it was common for Louise to respect authority. In fact, she was often rewarded for following the directives of her high school teachers, parents, and pastor. Louise understood that "doing as you are told" is a good thing. It was undoubtedly one of the reasons for which she was hired. Besides, Louise also knew that she could lose her job if she refused to obey a supervisor.

Although Donna had a certain degree of power over Louise Ogburn, Donna's role as an assistant manager was a long way from the top of the authority structure. She too was expected to obey orders from her superiors. This included the manager of the restaurant and an anonymous collection of McDonald's business executives known only as "corporate." Remember that Donna truly believed that her manager and corporate bosses were in contact with Officer Scott. And as a police detective, Officer Scott represented an additional dimension of authority. In Donna's mind, she was receiving instructions from a powerful collection of individuals in authoritative positions. Donna wanted to be a good employee. Donna wanted to be a good citizen. Why shouldn't she assist in the interrogation of Louise?

Authority is a powerful force. According to sociologist Max Weber (1864–1920), there are several different types of authority. Sometimes we obey an order because of tradition or custom. This is usually what is at work when we willfully follow the orders of our elders. Other times we might follow someone's commands because we are moved by their personal charisma or a belief that they have the power to transform our life. This is typical of individuals who are eager to take direction from a leader of a religious cult. But in modern society, most commands are obeyed because people believe in the legal authority of their superior. That is to say, they have accepted the rules of the organization or institution and see the person giving orders as a legitimate representative of a rational authority structure. According to Max Weber, an authority structure in the form of large bureaucracies is the most important defining feature of modern society.

Weber was a prolific early sociologist who developed his theories during the first part of the twentieth century. He did not live to see the efficient violence of World War II or the rise of dominant global corporations like McDonald's, but he would not have been surprised. Nor would he have likely been surprised by the widespread obedience to orders that resulted in the Nazi Holocaust, or the fast-food restaurant hoax that snared Donna Summers and others. According to Weber, the growth of large and influential "rational organizations" representing government, education, and work have a deep and troubling effect on the individual. In Weber's words, these increasingly bureaucratic institutions lead to "a parceling out of the soul." By this he meant that workers, students, and citizens are in danger of becoming cogs in a machine, grinding through a life devoid of authentic meaning and autonomous self-direction. In this way, authority is actually a form of domination. We may not feel coerced when we willingly follow rules or eagerly fall into line, but this is only because we have learned to accept the power of actors in certain organizational roles as legitimate.

QUESTIONING AUTHORITY

One of the most compelling and controlling authority structures in operation today is found in the U.S. armed forces. It is the largest, most complex, and most dominant military bureaucracy the world has ever known. It employs over 2.5 million people and spends over $700 billion a year. In fact, more than half of the world's military expenditures are made by the U.S. armed forces. No other country comes close to the United States in this regard.

A unique feature of a military bureaucracy is that it must train some of its employees to kill other human beings. Additional employees must also be trained to support the soldiers who are engaged in killing. This is not an easy task. Militaristic acts of violence must be normalized and distinguished from other "illegal" acts of killing. Taking the life of another person has to be configured as an honorable and virtuous act. To accomplish such a feat requires coordination and cooperation from many different institutions. Families, schools, churches, civic groups, and popular media must all work together to ensure that the military is represented as a morally righteous and ethical organization. For the most part, the effort is successful. But there are times when the military interpretation of killing is not accepted as legitimate.

I will never forget the day some years ago when I was teaching a seminar titled "The Sociology of Deviant Behavior." It was the first week of class, and as an initial assignment I had asked students to introduce themselves by sharing some background information—name, hometown, major, and so forth. Because the course topic was deviant behavior, I also asked the students to share some piece of biographical information that others might consider deviant. There were about fifteen of us in the class, and we were sitting around a large conference table. The first student admitted to being a chain smoker, the next student said he regularly smoked pot, and a third student confessed to having maxed out a large number of credit cards. Students were having a good time, giggling and teasing each other with mocked criticism and playful gasps of surprise. Then, near the end of the ice-breaking exercise, an older student calmly and deliberately announced that he had "committed an act of murder." The room fell suddenly silent. The tension was palpable, and I remember hearing the squeaking of a few chairs as other students began to fidget in their seats. After an uncomfortable period of eerie quiet, and sensing that no other information was going to be volunteered, I asked the student if he wanted to share the circumstances of his act. With a sincere and deliberate voice he softly replied, "It was about fifteen years ago in Vietnam. I shot and killed several people—strangers. The army gave me a medal for it . . . it felt like murder . . . it was murder."

Respecting the voice of authority and following the orders of a superior are easy. Others are usually in the same boat, doing the same thing, going with the flow, not making waves. In the military, noncompliance and resistance is the deviant act. Standing up to a senior military officer is what "crazy people" do. But after the killing, when the dead reappear in one's memory, soldiers are alone with images that may haunt them for the rest of their lives. Reconciling conflicting cultural messages is a challenge not easily met: "Thou shall not kill" does not come with a footnote or explanation of exceptions. My student, the Vietnam veteran, was as a young man a compliant and dutiful soldier. But the experience of killing, and the brutal deaths of his friends, transformed him and forever changed for him the meaning of war. For my student, the authority structure that legitimated war and sanctioned killing was unsuccessful.

As symbol users, we have the capacity to self-reflect, to contemplate and reevaluate. Every meaningful act becomes a part of our personal story, our biography, and our sense of who we are. We do not have the power to alter past acts, but we can alter our interpretation of the past. This is what many veterans of war struggle to achieve. This is what my student did when he redefined his wartime killing as murder. His transformation was a powerful personal experience, but it was a change that resulted from many complex social encounters with other people and other groups.

When the meaning of past acts is redefined, we also experience a redefinition of the self. With a new understanding of self comes a new possibility for resisting obedience to authority. We are not born with a permanent personality. Our personal preferences and behavioral tendencies are not etched in stone or coded onto our DNA. It is true that some people may more readily follow orders, respect authority, or leave bureaucratic leaders unchallenged. But this is not the result of a natural inner propensity. Social experience shapes us, and we are also capable of shaping our social experience. In this respect social groups are like a powerful river that carries us through life. Although we can never leave the river, it is possible to resist, struggle, and fight the direction of the current. Sometimes we can make a difference and sometimes we will fail. When we act alone, the chances of altering our course in the river will always be slim. To have any hope at all we need help from others. To resist the force of a group requires the force and support of other groups.

RESISTING AUTHORITY

For several years I volunteered to teach a few sociology courses at the Oregon State Penitentiary (OSP) in Salem, Oregon. At the time, OSP was the largest maximum security prison in the state. It housed over two thousand male inmates in an old brick-and-concrete fortress inside walls that have been standing since 1866. This was not a traditional college setting. The "classroom" was located at the top of several flights of stairs in a corner of the old prison. It held about twenty student desks in a cramped space. A small blackboard was located on a back wall, and a tiny side window looked down onto a corner of the recreational yard. Another large window allowed for a view of the main hallway where a corrections officer was usually stationed.

Prisons are an example of what sociologists call a "total institution." For inmates, each day of their life on the inside is planned, structured, controlled, and administered by the institution. When to eat, when to sleep, when to recreate, and when to visit are all determined by a professional staff. Clothing, food, and private possessions are nearly uniform. There is very little opportunity for personal discretion or the expression of individuality. The rules of the prison bureaucracy are intended to limit freedom, compel obedience, and prevent organized resistance. But even in this vastly restrictive and constraining environment, organized opposition to authority is possible. This was a lesson my students taught me one afternoon.

It was an unusually warm spring day, and I was not looking forward to spending two hours inside a prison. I had scheduled a midterm exam for the first hour and was hoping to correct some papers while the students worked on their tests. When I arrived that day, I remember the tiny prison classroom was hot and stuffy. I was feeling tired and a bit cranky, and the students also appeared restless and uncommonly serious. The usual joking, teasing, and loud banter was absent. The only noise came from a few hushed conversations near the center of the room. I attributed the changed demeanor to test anxiety.

As I fumbled through my file folder for the exams, I instructed the students to clear their desks. After distributing the midterm, I returned to the front of the classroom and noticed that no one was working on the exam. Instead, all eyes were focused on the middle of the room. One student, Jack Fischer,[6] had his hand up. This was unusual; the classroom atmosphere was informal, and students didn't need to raise their hands to speak. I sensed that something was up. Jack was a prison leader and was proud of his reputation as one of the strongest and toughest inmates at OSP—a reputation he bolstered by winning an amateur prison boxing title. "Professor Callero, when we have completed the exam, should we bring it to your desk?" I was puzzled; this wasn't our first exam, and this wasn't the first time I had taught these students. In a voice heavy with sarcasm I slowly and deliberately replied, "Yes, Jack, that it is what we usually do." Before I had completed my sentence, all twenty-five students abruptly stood up, marched in line to the front of the classroom, put their blank exams on my desk, turned, and walked in unison out the door and into the hallway.

I was caught off guard. I laughed nervously and mumbled something like "joke's over" and "OK, time to sit down." It didn't work. I felt a knot in my stomach, and I was starting to perspire. I am usually pretty calm in the classroom, and I rarely raise my voice, but I suddenly and unexpectedly found myself yelling at the inmates. "Get back in here! I'll flunk every one of you!" I had reached an emotional tipping point. My authority as a professor was being challenged, and I was pissed. As the last student left the room, I dashed into the hallway and tried to grab an inmate by the arm. I was now acting irrationally. For a moment I thought that maybe this was the beginning of an institutional uprising of some kind. That was before I noticed that the guard stationed outside the classroom was joking with several students while nodding in my direction.

I returned to the classroom, sat down, and tried to compose myself. I couldn't leave the building until the designated time for a shift change. I felt lost and powerless. After a few minutes of contemplation, the door to the classroom swung open and in marched Jack, followed closely by the other students. Jack was holding a piece of paper. He silently handed it to me before returning to his seat. He was joined by the other students who were now grinning with anticipation. On the paper was a short handwritten note:

> Dear Professor Callero,
> On the first day of class you explained to us that you would be grading on the curve and that the student with highest point total would receive

an "A." We asked you if everyone would get an A even if we all had a score of zero. You laughed and said yes but that it would never happen because students are too competitive. You also said that students would never have enough trust in each other to make such a plan succeed. We have just demonstrated to you that we are not like your other students. We did not intend to offend or anger you. This was about education. We are now prepared to complete the exam. Thank you for your commitment to our education.

The note was signed by every student in the class.

After the exam, the students spent close to an hour discussing their "demonstration of uniqueness." A good deal of the conversation was at my expense, but we also had time to review the sociology of the prank. How were they able to accomplish such a collective act of defiance? What made them different from my students on campus? It was no coincidence that the course title was "Self and Society"; my inmate-students had literally done their homework in preparation for the walk-out. After reviewing the published research on "revolutionary coalitions," they had determined that the right social conditions existed for them to succeed with their collective act of defiance. When they asserted that they were not like my other students, they were not referring to the fact that they were all male, that they all had serious criminal histories, or that they were on average about ten years older than a typical college student. They correctly recognized that individual characteristics have little effect on the emergence of a "revolutionary coalition." They had discovered that what matters most is social context. The distinctive circumstances of the prison environment are what made them unique and different from my other students.

To begin with, the group was relatively small. The smaller the group, the easier it is to develop and maintain a unanimous point of view. Second, there was maximum opportunity for member interaction and communication. The inmate-students shared more than time in the classroom; they were with each other for most of the day with ample opportunity to develop and discuss their plan. Third, because they lived inside the walls of OSP, they shared the same life experiences. Similar circumstances lead to common grievances and frustrations, which are usually the basis for defiance of authority. Fourth, research has shown that the anticipation of future contact with group members is an important factor in the maintenance of group solidarity. It is easier to deviate from the majority if you do not anticipate future contact with the other group members. As my inmate-students accurately pointed out, they were going to be living with each other for many years to come, and no one was interested in being known as the "asshole" or "snitch" who messed up the plan. Finally, leaders must emerge to facilitate and organize a common strategy. In this case, it was clear that Jack Fischer had played an important role in this regard. It was obvious that Jack was widely respected by the other students. He was smart, confident, and articulate. Plus, he was experienced in the ways of the prison, having spent more than half of his life behind bars. The fact that Jack was a physically powerful man also proved to be a key asset. After class one student told me in confidence that he considered breaking from the group, but he was afraid that he might "accidentally" fall down a flight of concrete stairs if he did. Inside the prison, violence and the threat of violence are essential resources for ensuring compliance and maintaining control. This is true for both inmates and the correctional staff.

This raises the question of whether it would be possible to form a revolutionary coalition of inmates large enough to successfully resist the bureaucratic authority of a maximum security prison. In a strictly hypothetical sense the answer is yes. But in the context of the OSP such an uprising is extremely unlikely. It is one thing for a small group of students to temporarily wrestle power from their professor, but it is quite another to seize control of an entire governmental institution. Even if all two thousand inmates were working in solidarity, they would still face the threat of violence from the state. Correctional officers and the Oregon National Guard have access to power in the form of trained personnel and deadly weapons. To succeed, the prison inmates would need to challenge the legitimacy of the state; in other words, they would need to have the support of the people of Oregon. As I said, this is very unlikely in the present historical context. Still, there is ample historical evidence that large-scale uprisings of this kind can in fact succeed. The most legendary example would be the "storming of the Bastille" in 1789, when revolutionary French demonstrators defied the French aristocracy and freed the few remaining inmates of the notorious prison. Revolutionary coalitions of this size and scale are obviously more complex and more challenging. We will take a closer look at this complicated social process later in chapter 7. For now we will continue to explore the more basic dynamics of small-group conflict.

SOLIDARITY AND CONFLICT BETWEEN GROUPS

One of the more important early studies of small-group conflict was conducted by Muzafer Sherif (1906–1988) and his colleagues. These researchers wanted to better understand the social forces that generated animosity between groups. In addition, they were also interested in examining several ideas about how to reduce intergroup hostility. To test their hypotheses they designed an ambitious social experiment that ran for nearly three weeks and involved twenty-two unsuspecting young boys.

The research took place during the summer of 1953 at an isolated Boy Scout camp in the middle of Robbers Cave State Park in Oklahoma. The boys who were recruited for the study had just completed the fifth grade and were roughly the same age—about eleven years old. Each participant was selected from a different grade school in Oklahoma City after a careful screening process to ensure "normal" physical and emotional development. The parents of the boys were told that their sons would be participating in a study of group interaction and team building under the supervision of a professional staff from the University of Oklahoma. Parents were also told that they would not be allowed to visit their child for the duration of the camp session. [7]

The experiment was organized into three distinct stages of about five to six days each. The goal of the first stage was to develop two distinct groups with relatively strong cohesion and solidarity. Several strategies were employed. First, the boys were assigned to one of two camp buses for the trip to the park. The buses left the city from separate locations, and as far as the campers knew, theirs was the only group going to the park. The two groups were also assigned to cabins far out of sight and sound of the other group. For the next several days, each group participated in a series of cooperative activities intended to build trust and enhance group identity. They went on hikes, pitched tents, planned cookouts, built a hideout, canoed, swam, and participated in a group treasure hunt. By the end of the first stage each group had a clear status hierarchy and informal authority structure. The boys also developed an obvious bond with their respective groups. They regularly used the pronouns "we" and "us," and they even adopted group names—the Rattlers and the Eagles, along with an identifying flag.

The second stage of the experiment was designed to create conflict between the Rattlers and the Eagles. Near the end of the first stage, limited and indirect contact was allowed, and the boys eventually learned that there was another cabin with boys their same age. At this point a competitive spirit and negative attitude toward the "out group" was already developing. The researchers enhanced the animosity between the two groups by organizing a tournament of games (baseball, football, tug of war) and judged competitions (a treasure hunt, cabin inspections, skits). The staff secretly manipulated the results of the judged competitions so as to ensure a spirited contest. The group with the most points at the end of the tournament was promised a large team trophy, individual medals, and brand-new pocket knifes. The prizes were displayed in a common dining area during the five days of the competition.

The competitive strategy proved to be very successful. In fact, the antagonism between the two groups became so severe and confrontational during this stage of the experiment that the staff had to intervene at several points to break up fist fights and prevent serious injury. The conflict occurred during and after the competitions and escalated from initial name calling and taunting to organized group violence. At one point after losing a game, the Rattlers stole the Eagles' flag and burned it in angry celebration. This desecration of the Eagles' symbol led to a series of retaliatory raids that eventually mushroomed out of control and required staff intervention. The researchers describe one such incident:

> After breakfast on Day 4, which the Eagles ate first, the Eagles prepared for the retaliatory raid that they had planned the previous night. After making sure that the Rattlers were in the mess hall, they started off, armed with sticks and bats. . . . The Eagles messed up the Rattlers' cabin, turning over beds, scattering dirt and possessions, and then returned to their cabin where they entrenched and prepared weapons (socks filled with rocks) for a possible return raid by the Rattlers. [8]

At the end of the tournament, after they had eked out a narrow victory on the very last event, the Eagles erupted with thunderous screams and tears of joy, jumping and hugging each other in celebration. The Eagles attributed their victory to the prayers they had recited during the tournament. The Rattlers, on the other hand, were visibly dejected and refused to eat in the same mess hall with the Eagles. Later that day the Rattlers engineered a final raid on the Eagles' cabin and stole the medals and knives that had been awarded to the victors.

The final stage of the experiment was designed to reduce intergroup hostility, and it was structured to test two different hypotheses. The first hypothesis concerned the possibility that increased social contact between the two groups would effectively reduce group friction. Thus, the staff arranged for seven different situations where the groups would come together in a noncompetitive environment. These were basic social gatherings such as a picnic, watching a movie, eating meals together, and shooting off fireworks on the Fourth of July. The researchers were not terribly surprised to find that none of the contact opportunities worked to diminish hostilities between the Ratters and the Eagles. In fact, the social contact situations actually became sites for more name calling and conflict.

The second hypothesis examined the idea that group harmony could be sustained if both groups worked together to achieve a common "superordinate goal." This was the central theoretical assumption of the experiment, and the researchers believed that cooperative projects could remove the animosity created by competition. Several different scenarios were created where group competition was replaced by a common problem that required the joint effort of both groups. For example, the first strategy involved a secret sabotage of the camp water supply. The staff then led both groups on an excursion to locate the malfunctioning pipe. Other situations included a common rope pull in which all of the boys had to cooperate to pull a truck that had "broken down," and a joint campout where camping gear had to be shared by both groups. The findings from these interventions were very positive. Positive interaction between group members increased, name calling and other antagonistic actions gradually ceased, seating patterns at the mess hall became more integrated, and on the bus ride home, the boys pooled their money so that everyone could afford a dessert treat. As a final testament to the success of introducing "superordinate goals," the staff observed that during the final half hour of the trip home, everyone from both groups stood close together near the front of the bus and joined collectively in singing a lively rendition of Oklahoma.

The Robbers Cave experiment was conducted over fifty years ago, but over the years similar hypotheses have been tested under different conditions and with different populations. The conclusions that we can draw from this body of research are central to understanding the force of small groups. Most importantly, we know that group conflict is less about individual personality or personal aggression and more about group structure and social context. Strong in-group solidarity strengthens the power of a group. When groups are cohesive there is both a trust among members as well as respect for authorities within the group. This can be a positive force for harmony and cooperation. However, if multiple groups find themselves in competition for valued resources, where one group's success is dependent upon another group's failure, conflict and aggression are likely. This suggests that diminution of war and other forms of group violence require changes in the "structural relations" between groups. As we saw in the Robbers Cave study, peace and cooperation can be transformed into anger and violence—and back again—by altering the social conditions under which people act. This was one of the more important points recognized by Karl Marx (1818–1883) more than one hundred years prior to the Sherif study. Marx, however, was focused on the social conditions created by a capitalist economic structure. He argued that the economic individualism of capitalism increases competition among workers and results in social conflict and the exploitation of working people. However, Marx also saw the potential of transforming competition into cooperation. When abused workers communicate and recognize their common fate, they can work together to create a more equitable and democratic economy. This, however, requires the development of a common group identity.

GROUP IDENTITY

As we have seen in the previous examples, groups are a powerful force in our lives. They touch us in many ways and through many different forms and sizes. They can be as large as a multinational corporation or as small as a friendship clique. Moreover, we have seen that groups are, on the one hand, a source of domination and exploitation, and, on the other hand, a resource for emancipation and justice. No matter how hard we might try, it is impossible to escape group membership. Humans are social animals, and we depend on groups for both physical and mental health. Even when we are socially isolated from others, groups continue to serve as the foundation of our identity. Consider, for example, a situation where you are approached by someone who asks, "Who are you?" It is generally not acceptable to reply, "I am happy," or "I am fifty-seven years old." Rather, we are expected to identify ourselves by signaling our group affiliations with a social placement such as "I am a professor" or "I am Kathleen's husband." Indeed, the most common response is to answer with one's name, as in "I am Peter

Callero." But a surname is simply a label for one's family membership and a place holder for other group identities.

In traditional, premodern societies, multiple group membership was relatively rare. One's clan or tribe was often the only available group identity. Work, religion, family, education, and recreation all occurred within the same group. To know one's tribe was to know one's identity. Today, however, societies are larger, more complex, and more "differentiated." This means that our lives are more likely to be lived in multiple locations with multiple groups. Thus, one's work is often separated from one's family; religion is typically separated from work; and education usually occurs in a public setting that is distinct from family, religion, and work. This division of our lives into different spheres is a defining feature of modern society and is associated with some important implications for group identity.

In the modern, post-traditional societies where most of us live today, we must contend with multiple groups and multiple group identities that may not be well integrated. This makes life more complicated and potentially stressful. Emile Durkheim (1858–1917), one of the founders of academic sociology, was particularly concerned about the negative consequences of an increasingly differentiated society. He felt that modern society, with its many competing social groups, was more disorganized than traditional society because it lacked a consistent set of common "social norms." For example, the workplace may promote values that are inconsistent with one's religious beliefs; one's faith community might advocate values that conflict with those being promoted in public schools; and some individuals could conceivably feel alienated from the political stance associated with their church, synagogue, or mosque. According to Durkheim, without a stable set of societal rules, deviant behavior, suicide, and a destructive form of egoism were more likely to take hold in modern society.

Suicide is no doubt an extreme response to the disconnected character of modern society. A more common experience is simply an overall increase in social confusion. With a range of competing group norms in society, we are forced to make choices on matters that used to be left to "tradition." But with many groups there can be many competing traditions. Moreover, in modern society there are many new groups that have not yet established much in the way of tradition. This can pose a difficult challenge for the average person, who may be left feeling uncertain about how to lead his or her life. Although the consistent and dominant set of norms found in a traditional society can be overly confining, restrictive, and limiting, they do provide an anchor and a compass so that people know who they are and where they are going. The freedom of modern society, on the other hand, can leave us feeling adrift at sea, searching for a safe and secure harbor—asking "Who am I?" and "What should I do?" This point was illustrated to me many years ago by a student of mine who was visiting from a country with a more traditional culture.

Hassan Saleh[9] arrived on our campus in the late 1980s with the intention of studying in the United States for a full academic year. His English-language skills were good, and he was looking forward to experiencing Western culture firsthand. Hassan was from the country of Yemen, which is located on the southern tip of the Saudi Arabian peninsula, just across the Red Sea from Africa. Like many other countries in the region, Yemen is considered an Islamic state. Close to 100 percent of the population is Muslim, and the laws of the country closely follow the recommendations of the Koran—the ancient Islamic holy book that is believed by devout Muslims to be the literal word of God.

There is very little separation of church and state in Yemen, and the Koran is used as a guide in education, family life, business, and government. As a consequence, alcohol is mostly banned, women are subordinated to men in marriage, and it is against the law for a Muslim in Yemen to convert to another religion. Unlike many of the other Persian Gulf countries, Yemen is not oil rich. Most citizens make their living using traditional practices of agriculture, and about half the population lives below the poverty line.

Even though Hassan thought of himself as a liberal thinker by the standards of his culture, he struggled to adapt to the social norms and expectations he encountered in the United States. Like many students who study abroad or attend college away from home, Hassan grew frustrated, became socially disengaged, and experienced a bout of depression. I could see it on his face the day he came to my office to tell me that he had decided to drop out of school and return to Yemen. He appeared sad and disappointed, and I wanted to cheer him up. "Don't be so hard on yourself," I said. "Your experience is quite common. Many college students often feel homesick." Hassan offered a polite smile but firmly rebuked my assumption: "I am not lonely, and I am not anxious to return home," he said. I was surprised by his response and thought that maybe something had been lost in translation, so I pursued the issue: "If it is not too personal, do you mind sharing with me your reason for leaving the United States?" Without a second of hesitation, Hassan exclaimed, "Too many choices!" I don't recall the exact words of the explanation that quickly followed, but I do remember that Hassan recited a litany of examples where he was expected to "choose." He complained about the long list of course offerings in the college catalog; the endless aisles of food in the supermarket; the infinite range of Western fashion styles, sizes, colors, and combinations; and a host of other options that require a decision on a regular basis. For Hassan, more choices meant more decisions, and more decisions meant more anxiety, less certainty, and less predictability. In Yemen, life was less complex and less surprising.

Hassan was right—modern society requires personal decisions on matters that never used to be an option. Where should I live? Whom should I live with? Where will I work? Should I marry? Should I have children? Do I believe in God? What faith tradition should I follow? Almost every aspect of life is now a possible decision. Even one's gender is a legitimate option for some people. In Yemen, the momentum of tradition took care of many decisions by removing choices and stabilizing expectations. The positive side of traditional society is a sustained feeling of psychological security. Hassan had a common and cohesive group identity in Yemen, but in America his traditional group identity was of little value. By moving from one social environment to another, Hassan found that the "psychological road maps" he brought from home were no longer useful. He was lost in a maze of new options, unique opportunities, confusing decisions, and endless selections. For Hassan, more choices felt less like freedom and more like prison.

When Hassan returned home, he no doubt found comfort in the familiar and predictable life of his family, friends, native language, and cultural traditions. Yet, with the spread of modern communication technologies and the increasing contact among world cultures, there is no guarantee that traditions will always remain secure. What would happen if the social environment in Hassan's homeland began to change? What if the security and predictability of life in Yemen was threatened by outside forces? What would happen if an entire society suddenly experienced the anxiety and insecurity that are associated with the loss of a traditional way of life? This, in fact, is what we are seeing today in many societies across the globe. It is especially evident in Southwest Asia. The same region of the world that felt secure and predictable to Hassan twenty years ago is now less stable and predictable, and more insecure and tense.

GROUP SOLIDARITY, GROUP IDENTITY, AND GROUP CONFLICT IN IRAQ

Not too far from Yemen, on the northern border of Saudi Arabia, sits the country of Iraq. Since the U.S.-led invasion of the country in 2003, more than one hundred thousand civilians have been killed, and it is estimated that another one million have suffered blast wounds and other serious conflict-related injuries. In early 2007, the country was averaging more than one hundred civilian deaths per day as a consequence of terrorist and military actions. By 2009, the death rate was down, but horrific accounts of killing were still a common occurrence throughout the country. During one week in February of 2009, Iranian news reported that a mother and her two children were killed by a roadside bomb; a bomb under a policeman's car killed his wife and his father; forty bodies were discovered in a mass grave; four boys were killed by a mortar shell; a university professor was shot leaving campus; a suicide bomber killed sixteen at a restaurant; and soldiers shot and killed an eight-year-old girl during a raid. And as I write these words in September 2012, the media are reporting another ninety-four deaths in a single day—all occurring as the result of car bombs and improvised explosives.

Violence of this magnitude over a sustained period of time is an immensely disruptive force. It upsets normal life, disturbs settled patterns of interaction, and has a profound effect on group identity. Imagine how you would react if family members and friends were violently killed; your job was lost and you had no prospects for future employment; work, food, water, and power were scarce; and foreign military personnel paroled your neighborhood in armored vehicles. Sociologists have known for some time that these circumstances lead groups to close ranks as they search for security among those they can trust. These social conditions are also associated with hostility toward outsiders and others that do not share one's language, religion, or customs.

This in fact is what we see today in Iraq. Iraq has not always been this violent or dangerous. In addition to the war between Iraqi insurgents and the occupying foreign powers, there is also a civil war that is being fought between ethnic and religious groups. Therefore, to understand group conflict in Iraq, we need to appreciate the major sources of group identity in the region. While it might be tempting to attribute the violence to individual beliefs associated with religion or culture, this would be a mistake. Complex social forces create the conditions that lead to organized death and destruction.

There are three major groups in Iraq that serve as the primary basis for group identity: the Kurds, the Sunni Arabs, and the Shi'a Arabs. The Kurds reside in the mountainous northern region of Iraq and make up about 20 percent of the country's population. Because the Kurds have their own unique language, political history, and traditions, they are considered to be a distinct ethnic group. Most Kurds do not feel a strong identity with Iraq and have been advocating for the establishment of their own country since the end of World War I.

Close to 100 percent of the Iraqi population is Muslim, but different religious traditions separate the Arab-speaking Iraqis into two distinct groups of believers. The Shi'a Arabs are the larger of the two sects, making up about 60 percent of the population. The Sunni Arabs are a religious minority, claiming slightly less than 40 percent of the believers. The split between the two sects can be traced back to the death of the prophet Mohammed in 632, but the current conflict between the Shi'a and Sunni Arabs has less to do with specific differences in religious belief and more to do with power and politics.

Since the end of World War II, the political history of Iraq has been shaped by a series of military coups, wars with neighboring countries, and a repressive political regime lead by Saddam Hussein. These violent episodes have helped to create and sustain group conflict within Iraq. Today we find Kurdish Muslims in conflict with Arab Muslims, and Shi'a Arabs in conflict with Sunni Arabs. It is a clash that has been made much worse by the U.S.-led invasion.

A recently published study of group identity and conflict in Iraq concludes that in-group solidarity is on the rise while hostility toward out-groups is at the highest level ever recorded.[10] These findings are based on a nationally representative sample of Iraqis interviewed in 2004 and again in 2006. When compared to similar surveys taken in other countries, the results are startling. Almost 90 percent of Iraqis voice negative attitudes toward "foreigners," saying they would not like to have them as neighbors. As expected, the greatest consensus was in rejecting "Westerners" from America and Europe. But Iraqis also showed unusually harsh attitudes toward other nationalities in their region, with 44 percent rejecting Jordanians, for example. By way of comparison, only 9 percent of Americans did not want to have a "foreigner or immigrant" as a neighbor.

As was noted above, people who feel threatened and insecure will often retreat to their in-group in search of security and comfort. This results in greater in-group cohesion, but it also works to narrow and radicalize negative beliefs about outsiders as fear of the unknown increases. The targets of intolerance can be wide ranging and may include local groups as well as "foreigners and immigrants." Thus, in Iraq, negative attitudes toward women, homosexuals, and atheists have also shown a dramatic increase in recent years. As in-groups close ranks against outsiders, conformity to group norms increases. In addition, loyalty and obedience become important values while independence is discouraged. In general, groups become more traditional and conservative. This in fact is what researchers found in their survey of the Iraqi people. When asked to evaluate a list of common values, Iraqi Arabs ranked "obedience" higher than the publics of any other country. They were also among the very lowest in emphasizing "independence," while also ranking "religious faith" higher than any other nation surveyed. In contrast, the Iraqi Kurds, who reside in a relatively isolated region of Iraq that is significantly more peaceful, gave answers that were on average much less extreme on all of these indicators—although still high compared to other nations.

Conflict between Shi'a Arabs and Sunni Arabs has a long history. But the current level of extraordinary violence was sparked by the U.S.-led invasion and continues to be fueled by the U.S. occupation. The disruptions caused by the military incursion created unpredictable economic and political futures and worked to polarize the two religious groups. Only 33 percent of Iraqis say that they "strongly trust" other Iraqi ethnic groups, while 86 percent say that they strongly trust their own group. We expect to see preferences for one's own group, but the evidence suggests that the distinction between groups in Iraq is increasing along with the levels of hostility and violence. It is a social process that will no doubt continue as long as foreign military forces are present.

Historical evidence and experiments with small groups indicate that it is possible to reduce intergroup conflict. While differences between groups are inevitable, we should not assume that difference alone leads to conflict. Violent group conflict cannot be understood in terms of individual pathology or human nature; it demands a sociological analysis that recognizes the complexity of forces at work in multiple groups and at multiple levels. We are all members of many groups that overlap, intermingle, vary in importance, and come together to shape our identity. In the next chapter we will see how two very different types of groups, our family and our social class, are of particular significance.

Chapter Four

Family Matters

The Power of Social Class

It is a typical evening at the Simpson house. Mother Marge is tending to baby Maggie while brother Bart and sister Lisa are engaged in an animated argument over money. Homer, the family patriarch, appears oblivious to the debate as he sits transfixed in front of the television. Then, with sudden inspiration, he snaps out of his trance to interject some fatherly wisdom: "Listen to me kids! If you want to make good money you have to work for it. Now shut up; they are about to announce the lottery numbers."

Homer Simpson is possibly the most popular cartoon character in American history. As patriarch of the lovable Simpson clan, he is devoted to his family, committed to his job as a nuclear power plant safety inspector, and proud of his country. Like many American men, Homer spends much of his leisure time at home, wants to keep his family safe, occasionally attends religious services, and may at times be a little self-centered. But more than anything else, Homer represents the dilemma of American individualism—he lives in a society where individual effort is promoted as a cultural value, but hard work is not always equally rewarded.

The Simpsons are a caricature of the American working-class family, and Homer's exaggerated perspective is humorous because we can recognize an element of sad truth in much of what he has to say. In this way, the Simpson family satirizes both the promise and the reality of

85

life in America. Homer may be lazy, borderline alcoholic, and incompetent, but his daughter Lisa is brilliant, and son Bart, while clearly a delinquent, also shows promise. Viewers can only wonder what the future holds for the Simpson children.

If the Simpson children experience an American economy where hard work and individual effort lead to opportunity and success, Bart and Lisa should be able to realize "intergenerational mobility" (move up the economic ladder) and live a life with greater wealth, job security, and social influence (the potential of baby Maggie also looks promising). But if their cartoon society reflects an American economy where one's family background determines the likelihood of future success, Bart, Lisa, and Maggie will be stymied in their struggle to get ahead of their parents, and hopes of an upper-middle-class life will remain an unfulfilled dream.

The relationship between family background and a child's economic future is a fundamental sociological question. How important is family? What role does individual effort play? Can hard work overcome the disadvantages of family background? Does family background impose an unfair and undemocratic benefit to children of the wealthy? While most Americans acknowledge that "family matters" when it comes to future success, many more believe that individual effort and hard work is the most important factor in "getting ahead in life." Compare, for example, the following results from a recent survey of the U.S. adult population (table 4.1).

Table 4.1.

How important do you think coming from a wealthy family is for getting ahead in life?

Essential	11 percent
Very important	33 percent
Somewhat important	40 percent
Not very important	10 percent
Not at all important	6 percent
Don't know/no answer	1 percent

How important do you think hard work is for getting ahead in life?

Essential	46 percent
Very important	41 percent
Somewhat important	11 percent
Not very important	2 percent
Not at all important	—

Source: *New York Times* Poll, 2005, as reported in *Class Matters*, by correspondents of the *New York Times* (New York: Times Books, 2005). Totals may not reach 100 percent due to rounding.

Only 11 percent of Americans think that coming from a wealthy family is "essential" for getting ahead in life. Many more Americans believe that "hard work" is the key to success. This optimism with regard to individual effort sets us apart from citizens in other capitalist countries. Compare, for example, the results in table 4.2 from a recent survey asking respondents if they agree that hard work guarantees success.

Table 4.2.

Which statement comes closer to your own views, even if neither is exactly right? Most people can succeed if they are willing to work hard; or hard work is no guarantee of success for most people.

	Can succeed if working hard (%)	Success is not guaranteed (%)	Neither, both DK/NA (%)
United States	77	20	3
Britain	57	41	2
Spain	56	43	1
Germany	51	48	1
France	46	54	0
Italy	43	46	11
Greece	43	51	6

Source: Pew Research Center for the People and the Press, July 2012.

This should come as no surprise. As we saw in chapter 1, the myth of economic individualism is a dominant theme in American culture. Americans have a disproportionate confidence in the ability of the poor and underprivileged to someday "make it" in America. In fact, faith in "upward mobility" appears to be on the increase in the United States. Consider the survey responses in table 4.3 recorded over a period of twenty-eight years.

Table 4.3.

Do you think it is possible to start out poor in this country, work hard, and become rich?

	Possible (%)	Not possible (%)	DK/NA (%)
1983	57	38	5
1996	70	27	3
2011	75	24	1

Source: Correspondents of the *New York Times*, *Class Matters* (New York: Times Books, 2005), and CBS/*New York Times* poll, 2011.

From a sociological perspective, there is great irony in these survey findings. While more people today believe that movement from poverty to prosperity is possible, the evidence indicates that it is in fact becoming more difficult to make such a leap. Over the past twenty-five years we have seen a hardening of the class structure. The river that used to move boats from a lower class to an upper social class is freezing up. This is especially true at the top and the bottom where the children of the poorest Americans are more likely to stay poor and the children of the richest Americans are even more likely to remain rich. The inheritance of wealth, income, and education is more common today than it was for previous generations, and the gap between the poorest and the richest has been growing. This means that the distance needed to travel before one can "get ahead" has also increased. Moreover, contrary to popular perception, the chances of "moving on up" are not any better in the United States than in other industrialized nations; countries such as Canada, Sweden, Finland, and Norway actually have higher rates of social class mobility.

The Simpsons first appeared on television in 1987, and over the past twenty-five years Bart, Lisa, and Maggie have maintained their original cartoon age. But if they were somehow able to develop and mature in the same manner as a typical American family, we would most likely see the Simpson children living their adult lives at or below the social class level occupied by Homer and Marge. In the real world, social class position is not simply a matter of hard work, intelligence, or moral values. There are both barriers and resources associated with one's family that serve to block or facilitate the path to economic prosperity. To understand why and how "family matters," we need to understand the power and force of social class. Remember, in a capitalist economy, social class is essentially about one's location in the production process. Are you producing things and selling your labor for a wage, or do you control and manage a large business? This is an oversimplification, of course, and most of us can recognize that our class position is more complex. Social class is also reflected in the way our lives are led outside of the workplace. For illustrative purposes we can begin with a closer look at the lives of two young boys who come from two very different social classes.

ALEXANDER WILLIAMS

Alexander Williams is a typical ten-year-old boy who enjoys sports, learning about cars, and debating the relative power of the X-Men. Alexander is a handsome African American with an engaging smile and a self-confident demeanor. He is taller and thinner than most of his fourth-grade classmates and, according to a teacher, "gets along with everybody."

Alexander lives with his mother and father in a large, six-bedroom house in an upper-middle-class, urban neighborhood. He attends a private school where the vast majority of children are white. Both of Alexander's parents graduated from a private liberal arts college. His mother works in a management position for a large corporation, and his father works as a trial lawyer for a small firm. Together, the couple earns well over $200,000 annually. In economic terms Alexander's family is clearly privileged.

A typical week for Alexander is similar to that of children who share his social class position. Weekends and afternoons are packed with structured group activities that are organized and led by adults. These include piano lessons, guitar lessons, choir practice, and Sunday school. He also participates in multiple sports—soccer, tennis, baseball, and basketball—that require fees, equipment, and travel. Despite being an only child, Alexander leads a busy and hectic life that demands a close monitoring of the family calendar—lest he miss an event or need to adjust overlapping activities. His parents are equally busy with work that often requires either out-of-town trips or late evenings at the office. The Williams family may not arrive home until 9:00 p.m. on some evenings. When free time is available after dinner, Alexander is expected to complete his homework, while time in front of the television is strictly controlled by his mother. The busy pace is normal for Alexander, and although he is often tired, he also complains of being "bored" when there is downtime between activities. There are few playmates and no relatives in Alexander's neighborhood. His grandparents and cousins live out of state.

Mr. and Mrs. Williams believe that the music lessons, after-school activities, and sport teams play an important role in developing Alexander's talents. For the same reason, they often view everyday conversations as an opportunity to expand Alexander's reasoning skills and a chance to extend their son's vocabulary. For example, once when Alexander was completing a homework assignment, he joked about copying material from a reference book. His mother explained that such an act would be considered "plagiarism," and his father commented on the possibility of being sued for violating "copyright protection."

At times Alexander can be self-centered, argumentative, and disrespectful to adults. He will sometimes ignore his parents' instructions or persist in negotiating his own position. These acts either are met with laughter by his parents or result in verbal warnings. The Williamses do not hit, spank, or threaten to use physical force when disciplining Alexander.

TYREC TAYLOR

Tyrec Taylor is also African American, nine years old, and in the fourth grade. He is small for his age but can be very assertive and self-confident with his friends. Unlike Alexander Williams, Tyrec comes from a relatively poor working-class family. The Taylors live in a four-bedroom rented house in a predominantly black urban neighborhood. There are numerous small shops and a bus line within easy walking distance. Tyrec lives with his mother, thirteen-year-old sister, Anisha, and eighteen-year-old stepbrother, Malcolm. Mr. and Mrs. Taylor are separated, and Tyrec's father lives about fifteen minutes away in the same city. Although living outside the home, Mr. Taylor maintains close contact with the family, visits at least once a week, and speaks to his children by phone almost daily. Mrs. Taylor is a high school graduate and works full time as a secretary. Her job only pays about $20,000 annually, but it has the benefit of health insurance. Mr. Taylor never completed high school and is currently unemployed. The family owns an older car that is often broken down and unreliable.

Tyrec attends a racially integrated public grade school near his home. He is an average student, receiving mostly Bs and Cs. Compared to Alexander Williams, Tyrec's life is much less structured and controlled by formal activities. Most of his time after school and on weekends is spent playing outside with a group of neighborhood boys or watching television with family members. Like many children from working-class families, Tyrec has regular contact with extended family members who live close by, including grandparents, as well as several aunts and cousins. It is not unusual for Tyrec to spend Saturday morning helping his great-grandmother with chores around her house, and he will often spend the night with his cousins, who live just around the corner. Tyrec loves to play sports and is especially fond of football. Almost all of his athletic competition occurs in the streets or on the playground with a group of five to ten boys. He did play on an organized football team for one season, but Mrs. Taylor found this to be a demanding commitment of time and energy and she did not encourage him to continue. Tyrec, himself, was often torn between football practices and playing with his neighborhood buddies.

Tyrec has learned that all adults deserve automatic respect, and he shows deference to women by prefacing their names with "Miss." His mother establishes clear boundaries of acceptable behavior, including no cussing, homework before after-school play, and in the house at a set time in the evening. There are also limits to how far Tyrec is allowed to travel from his house. But within these confines, Tyrec experiences a relative degree of freedom and unsupervised discretion. If he violates a family rule, he is usually restricted to home. Mrs. Taylor also believes that a periodic spanking can be helpful in maintaining good behavior.

Compared to Alexander Williams, Tyrec spends much less time in conversation with adults. When interaction does occur, it is more likely to consist of a series of commands and instructions as opposed to explanations and verbal wrangling. Tyrec is also less tired, doesn't complain of boredom, and rarely engages in arguments with adults. He does, however, have energetic disagreements with his friends. These typically involve a dispute over the rules of a game or the proper enforcement of a playground violation.

THE RELATIONSHIP BETWEEN CLASS AND FAMILY LIFE

The descriptions of Alexander and Tyrec are taken from an important study of family life conducted by sociologist Annette Lareau. Professor Lareau's work is part of a much larger body of research that explores the way in which social class shapes our everyday life experiences and controls access to valuable societal resources. [1] This tradition of scholarships asks, Why are children of the upper middle class likely to be upper middle class as adults? Why are children of the poor and working class likely to be poor or working class as adults? Are there class differences in the way children are raised? Do these differences in child-rearing practices have an effect on future class position?

Notice that these questions assume that one's economic standing as an adult is not simply the result of hard work, perseverance, and individual initiative. As was noted above, the sociological evidence clearly shows that the class position of one's family is the best predictor of one's own class position as an adult. If individual attributes were the most important factor in determining one's economic future, we would have to conclude that poor and working-class people are less intelligent, less skillful, or simply don't work as hard as members of the upper class. While most Americans would probably reject this position when framed in such a blunt manner, there are plenty who remain committed to this class myth despite evidence to the contrary. Thus, many adults in the upper classes attribute their success to superior individual skills and attributes. Donald Trump, for example, routinely dispenses advice in his books and television shows on how to get rich and gain power. Yet "the Donald" rarely mentions that he inherited an enormous amount of wealth from his father. As the saying goes, "He was born on third base but acts like he hit a triple." This is not to say that social class position is completely determined by one's family. There are many individual exceptions to this social pattern. But the identification of an exception, or even a large number of exceptions, is not sufficient to dismiss a social fact.

Consider, for example, the link between cigarette smoking and lung cancer. It is true that not every regular smoker will develop cancer. My own grandmother, for example, smoked for fifty years before she quit, and today at the age of ninety-nine she is cancer free. Nevertheless, it would be foolish to conclude on the basis of individual exceptions that smoking is not a cause of cancer. When we look at the historical evidence, across a large sample of smokers, we find that smokers do indeed have a much higher probability of contracting the disease—as much as twenty times higher than nonsmokers. The same logic of probability holds true for the transmission of class. Not everyone born into a poor family is destined to remain poor, and there are examples of children born into upper-class families who end up living working-class lives as adults. But the most likely result, the one with the greatest chance of occurring, is for children to end up in the same class position as their parents. [2]

Why is this? What is it about family life that influences future class position? Why, for example, does Alexander Williams have a much greater chance of living a wealthier and more privileged adult life than Tyrec Taylor? To answer this question, we must first abandon the myth of individualism and recognize that family and social class are important parts of a much larger social system. Even though Tyrec and Alexander live in the same country, speak the same language, and are equally healthy, curious, and energetic, they inhabit dissimilar social worlds. They come from two distinct social classes, and class is much more than a measure of how much money someone has in a bank account. Sociologist Stanley Aronowitz summarizes this point well:

> In every crevice of everyday life we find signs of class difference; we are acutely aware that class plays a decisive role in social relations. Professionals and managers do not mingle much with service or industrial workers, immaterial workers of all sorts are rarely in the company of blue-collar workers, and none of the above socialize with the poor, working or not. In sum, black or white, there is little blending of people from sharply disparate economic backgrounds. They inhabit different neighborhoods. . . . Different socioeconomic groups attend different churches, increasingly send their kids to different schools, and have different forms of leisure-time activity. [3]

Once again, it is important to emphasize here that differences in family structure and lifestyle do not define social class. Social class is defined by differences in power that have their origin in the economy. Variation in child rearing is related to social class, but these differences do not create social classes.

Some people prefer to think of social classes as different rungs on a very long ladder where individuals climb independently toward the top. According to this analogy, people find themselves on different rungs (in different classes) at various stages in life due to individual effort and skill. Consequently, those who manage to "achieve" a place in the upper class (upper rung) are assumed to be deserving and superior in some way. This, however, is an inaccurate analogy. A social class is a discrete group, socially segregated from other social classes, where members usually share a common social history as well as a predictable future. A more appropriate analogy, therefore, would be to think of two different elevators. One elevator might have a history of mechanical problems, rarely operates in a predictable manner, and often stalls on the first or second floor. This is the elevator reserved for poor and working-class families. A second elevator has a history of regular maintenance, moves swiftly to the top of the building, and hardly ever suffers from mechanical failure. This elevator is reserved for families of the upper class. Tyrec and Alexander are not competing against each other on the same ladder; instead, they are with their families on two different elevators. The real competition occurs between classes not individuals.

CLASS COMPETITION

We should not assume that social classes are completely independent of each other. This is a limitation of the elevator analogy. In the real world, social classes are related through an inherent competition. This means that the economic "success" of upper-class families often occurs at the expense of families lower in the class system. Consider, for example, the slave economy of the American South before the Civil War. The ruling class of slave owners reaped enormous profit from their plantations where they grew sugar, cotton, tobacco, and rice. But this profit was at the expense of the families who were held in captivity and brutally exploited for their labor. The "success" of the slave-holding class was at the expense of the slave families. Today we no longer have a slave-based economy in the United States. However, it is still true that much of the agricultural industry benefits from the exploitation of farmworkers. Thus, in most states, farmworkers are excluded from laws that were written to protect workers from abuse, including laws dealing with child labor, hourly wages, and the right to join a union.

The competition between classes is not limited to the agricultural industry either. Any "successful" business owner recognizes that profit can be increased by limiting the wages and benefits of employees. Wal-Mart, for example, is the largest employer in the United States, and the owners of the company, the Walton family, are among the wealthiest individuals in the world. But the "success" of the company has been at the expense of their "associates," who earned an average of $8.81 an hour in 2010, which for a family of four is below the national poverty level. It should come as no surprise that companies like Wal-Mart fiercely resist the unionization of workers and lobby against increases in the minimum wage.

When one social class benefits from the exploitation of another social class, there is always the chance that the exploited class will revolt and demand greater equality and justice. If the ruling class is successfully entrenched in power, inequality and exploitation are widely assumed to be normal, natural, and inevitable. But if an oppressed class begins to agitate for change, the ruling class must learn to defend its position of domination and develop reasons and arguments to justify the system of exploitation. This is what we saw in the United States when the slave economy came under attack. Southern slave owners and other white families who benefited from slavery argued that the slaves were actually better off working on the plantation than they would be in the "jungles" of Africa. Slavery, therefore, was said to be a "step up" from the life of a "savage." Pro-slavery elites argued that "the negro" was not as intelligent, not as civilized, and not fully human. Accordingly, they argued that without the protection and direction of the slave master, the slave would be incapable of making it in the free world. The ruling class also argued that the emancipation of the slave would have a disastrous effect on the nation's economy and so all social classes would be worse off if the institution of slavery were to be dissolved. But perhaps the most powerful and often repeated justification was that slavery was consistent with God's will.[4]

Books, pamphlets, newspaper editorials, school lectures, and church sermons regularly and forcefully reviewed the biblical evidence in support of slavery. Both the Old and New Testament were scoured for evidence from scripture that could be used to demonstrate that slavery was consistent with a Christian life. For example, the Reverend Richard Furman, after articulating the many examples of slavery in the Bible, concluded that slavery "is not a sin (or) a moral evil. For God never did and never will authorize men to commit sin." Furman reasoned that if Christ opposed slavery, he would have explicitly denounced it in his teachings. Frederick Dalcho, writing at the same time, went even further and argued that it was actually sinful for slaves to revolt or in any way resist their state in life since, according to the New

Testament, "obedience, submission, (and) subjection to a bad as well as a good master" is required.[5] This reading of scripture required a selective and literal interpretation of the Bible, but it was consistent with the Evangelical Christianity that dominated the culture of the region. Many southern Christians actually believed that slavery was a necessary burden that served God's glory by bringing "spiritual salvation" to the otherwise heathen Africans.

The church was not the only institution that contributed to the cultural legitimation of slavery. The practitioners of medicine also used the prestige and authority of their discipline to argue for the scientific "evidence" that slavery was justified and that slaves benefited from their subservient status. This was the argument developed by Dr. Samuel Cartwright, a highly respected and influential surgeon who was considered an expert on the health of African Americans. In 1851, Dr. Cartwright published a widely read article in the *New Orleans Medical and Surgical Journal* in which he described a new disease called "drapetomania" that was found only among African Americans. According to Dr. Cartwright, drapetomania is an affliction that "induces the Negro to run away from service, [and] is as much a disease of the mind as any other species of mental alienation, and much more curable, as a general rule." In other words, slaves who attempted to escape from their captors were in fact showing symptoms of drapetomania. The cure for drapetomania, according to Dr. Cartwright's research, included the physical beating and whipping of the patient.

Doctors, preachers, teachers, politicians, and other representative leaders of the ruling class were instrumental in reaffirming, justifying, and legitimating an exploitative class system. As members of the ruling class, they benefited from the status quo and stood to lose if "the rules of the game" were to suddenly change. The economics of slavery were supported by a set of racist beliefs that favored the ruling class. By today's standards, the culture of slavery is viewed as illogical, unreasonable, and immoral, and we can clearly see the exploitative nature of this particular class relationship. But it is important to recognize that we still live in a society structured by class, and more importantly, a dominant ruling class continues to justify and legitimate its position of authority with a set of cultural beliefs.

Without the advantage of historical perspective it can be hard to recognize class-based inequality in our present lives, but it would be naive to assume that class exploitation has somehow disappeared. While African Americans continue to suffer from the cultural legacy of racism, the more fundamental source of inequality today is not the economics of slavery but rather the economics of capitalism. With every new economic system comes a new set of beliefs for justifying inequality as well as a new cultural system that protects the privileged position of the ruling class.

CULTURAL CAPITAL

Without historical perspective our vision is fuzzy and evidence of exploitation is hard to see. We can certainly recognize class differences when it comes to income and material wealth (Tyrec and Alexander certainly don't live equal economic lives), but it is a challenge to appreciate the noneconomic forces associated with inequality. To understand how class inequality is reproduced and legitimated under capitalism, we must distinguish between "economic capital" and "cultural capital."

Economic capital refers to the material resources that are accumulated, invested, and traded under capitalism. One has to be relatively rich before gaining access to economic capital. While middle-class Americans may have cash in the bank and might even own a car or a house, these assets are not considered economic capital unless they are invested or traded for profit. For wealthy Americans, economic capital usually takes the form of stocks, bonds, securities, land, rental properties, and ownership in various business ventures. Even though the United States is considered one of the wealthiest nations in the world, most Americans have very little economic capital. This is because economic capital is highly concentrated in the hands of the very rich. The top 1 percent of households in the United States own 40 percent of all financial capital (wealth minus housing) and 57 percent of all business equity (wealth in the form of a business). The top 10 percent of households own 90 percent of the stock, bonds, and business equity. Thus, Jim Walton, whose father founded Wal-Mart, has economic capital worth more than $16 billion. Jim's brother, Robson, is also worth $16 billion, as is their sister, Alice. Most economic capital passes from one generation to the next through family inheritances. However, unlike the Walton family, over 90 percent of Americans receive no inheritance at all.[6]

In contrast to economic capital, cultural capital is much more difficult to recognize and quantify. When sociologists talk about cultural capital, they are referring to a range of different skills, habits, preferences, types of knowledge, and lifestyle that come to be associated with

people who share different class positions in society. For example,
Tyrec and Alexander will inherit more than different amounts of economic capital from their parents; they will also inherit different ways of
speaking, different accents, different vocabularies, and different tastes
for food, music, and art. There will also be differences in fashion, table
manners, and posture in the presence of others. All of these qualities
are examples of cultural capital. Forms of cultural capital are often
misinterpreted or misrecognized as natural individual differences, or
"personality," when in fact they are qualities learned at a very early age
from relatives, friends, neighbors, and others that one has contact with
on a regular basis. Because social classes are geographically and socially segregated, they tend to exhibit distinct types of cultural capital.

For example, research has demonstrated important differences between classes in terms of how children play. Children from working-
class and poor families tend to spend much less time in formal after-
school activities than do children from upper- and middle-class families. This difference in leisure time experience cultivates different sets
of skills and competencies that become part of one's stock of cultural
capital. Children such as Tyrec, for instance, are more likely to direct
and control their own play time in the absence of direct supervision of
an adult. As a result they are more likely to develop skills for managing
and resolving conflict between peers. Working-class children, especially boys, also learn how to physically defend themselves if necessary.
When Tyrec hangs out with neighborhood kids, he engages in a number
of different games and competitions that are often invented, initiated,
and concluded by children on their own time. Informal neighborhood
play will also include children from a much larger age range than one
would typically find in the formal athletic leagues that structure Alexander's play. In contrast to the parent-organized activities that characterize middle-class play, working-class and poor children are free from
the performance evaluations of adults. Without coaches, referees,
judges, and team rankings, children such as Tyrec are less likely to be
formally assessed and appraised in their activities. As a result, Tyrec is
more adept at managing his unstructured time and shows more creativity and independence in this aspect of his life.

This is in stark contrast to adult-organized activities that dominate
Alexander's life and the life of other upper-middle-class children. Alexander is developing a different set of life skills, preferences, and
competencies—different forms of cultural capital. Because his leisure
time is formally controlled and structured by adults, Alexander spends

much more time in equal conversation with adults than does Tyrec. He is also learning that he is entitled to attention from adults. While Tyrec may have more versatility and experience in dealing with peer conflict and the creative organization of peer relationships, Alexander is more at home and at ease in an upper-middle-class world of grown-ups in professional occupations that hold positions of power. Thus when Alexander paid a visit to the family doctor for a physical exam, he was encouraged by his mother to prepare questions in advance and to seek clarification if he was confused. Several times during the exam Alexander confidently joked with his physician, and at another point he assertively corrected his mother. What might be viewed by Tyrec's family as disrespectful behavior on the part of the child was instead proudly framed by Alexander's mother as evidence that her son was learning self-confidence and assertiveness.

Unlike economic capital, everyone possesses cultural capital. We all have skills, tastes, accents, habits, and forms of knowledge. But even though cultural capital is evenly distributed across different social classes, some types of cultural capital are valued more than others. Some forms of cultural capital elicit more respect and deference from others; some forms of cultural capital are associated with "intelligence" and "good taste"; and most important of all, some forms of cultural capital provide access to greater amounts of economic capital. Not surprisingly, the cultural capital associated with elite and upper-middle-class families tends to be more highly valued in every society; it opens more doors, attracts more positive attention, and is used as the criteria for grading and evaluating worth inside formal institutions. No institution is more critical and influential in this regard than the school.

The form of cultural capital that is valued and privileged by schoolteachers and school administrators is upper-middle-class cultural capital. It is imbedded in the curriculum and reflected in the standards for formally and informally assessing children. This should not be too surprising; after all, teachers, school administrators, and other education professionals usually come from middle-class families, and teachers who are hired to teach at elite private schools are even more likely to share the same upper-class background as their students. For many middle-class children, school feels familiar and comfortable. But for working-class and poor children, the styles of interacting and the expectations of teachers may seem foreign and confusing. When a child is engaged in the lesson and confidently interacting with the teacher, he or she is positively evaluated. If the child appears uncertain or unwilling to participate in interactions with adults, the teacher's evaluation and expectations may be less positive. Alexander's cultural capital has more value in the classroom, while Tyrec's cultural capital has more value on the playground.

The different value attached to a student's cultural capital is significant because a teacher's expectations influence student success. An important line of research has demonstrated that when teachers expect students to succeed, they have a greater chance at success; and when teachers expect students to perform poorly, they are more likely to fail. This influence of teacher expectations, called the self-fulfilling prophecy, was first exposed in 1968 when Robert Rosenthal and Lenore Jacobson published the results of their famous experiment.[7] The study took place at a grade school in a working-class neighborhood. At the start of the school year, every student was administered an "intelligence test" that produced a single score known as the "intelligence quotient" (IQ). When teachers were shown the results of the test, they were told that the test was also able to identify students who showed the greatest "growth potential" and were thus most likely to make progress during the academic year. Approximately 20 percent of the students in each grade were identified in this manner as showing unique learning potential. In truth, however, the test was simply a measure of knowledge and academic skill. It did not measure potential or likelihood of improvement. The researchers deliberately misled the teachers and randomly identified some of the students as "bloomers" to see if this expectation would have an effect on student success. At the end of the school year the same test of academic knowledge and skill was re-administered to the students. The results were startling. The students who had been randomly identified as having more potential actually did show more improvement in comparison to the other students. The gains were especially pronounced for first- and second-graders. In subsequent years comparable studies in different schools and for different levels of education have produced similar results.

Cultural capital influences teacher expectations by providing symbols or markers of stereotypes for "academic potential." Students who display confident interaction styles, middle-class vocabularies, or even a more stylish wardrobe can signal value and can lead teachers to the expectation of future success. Clearly, cultural capital has important symbolic power that can produce subtle but significant effects. In this way, schools can actually work to sustain and even exacerbate class differences. In a society where the amount and quality of formal education is closely linked to economic success, schools serve as critical "gatekeepers" by monitoring and controlling access to pathways between social classes. Many working-class children who struggle academically and fall behind their middle-class schoolmates are at a disadvantage because their cultural capital is considered less valuable. With an overly individualistic view of the world, different forms of cultural capital are misinterpreted as differences in "academic potential" or inherent differences in "IQ." Some people may even wrongly conclude that early childhood differences in school performance are based on genetics—an interpretation that is dangerously close to the racist and sexist explanations of the eugenics movement that was discussed in chapter 2.[8]

There are real differences of academic success that separate social classes. But these differences are not the result of individually inherited intellectual abilities; rather, they are the result of socially created separations that give an advantage to one class over another. This does not mean that there is no such thing as individual variations. It would be silly to argue that the differences separating Tyrec and Alexander, for example, are due solely to social background. There are certainly individual idiosyncrasies and personal peculiarities that distinguish the two boys. After all, brothers and sisters from the same social environment often display unique qualities, skills, styles, and competencies. It would be wrong to conclude that something called "society" determines our behavior. This is an unsophisticated and oversimplified interpretation of human action. Nevertheless, in the complex and often unpredictable dynamic of social interaction, consistent, observable patterns do emerge. Social forces may not determine our unique qualities, but social forces do shape the context within which specific differences are given value over others.

Think of society as a game or a sport with a set of rules and objectives. Different societies have different rules in the same way that different games or sports have different rules. The sport of American football, for example, is structured in such a way that physically powerful individuals have an advantage. Someone who weighs three hundred pounds and can run forty yards in 4.9 seconds is more likely to succeed in football than someone who weighs 125 pounds no matter what his or her speed. Size matters in football because the rules of the sport are "rigged" in favor of large bodies.[9] Outside of football, in a game with a different set of rules, a large body may be a disadvantage. In the sport of cross-country, or in a marathon race, for example, the athlete who weighs 125 pounds will have a greater chance at success. In other words, the value of a particular attribute or skill is dependent upon the rules that govern a game or a society. In this regard, it is very important to recognize that rules are neither random nor natural. They are socially constructed and enforced by those in society who have more power. In a game organized by physically powerful people, the rules of the game will likely be set to favor physically powerful people. In the same way, in a society ruled by those with more economic capital, the rules of the game will be set to favor those with more economic capital.

SOURCES OF CULTURAL CAPITAL

To understand why and how upper- and middle-class forms of cultural capital come to be valued over lower- and working-class forms of cultural capital, we first need to take a closer look at the origins of cultural capital. How do we explain class differences in cultural capital? Earlier in this chapter we said that class differences reflect common qualities passed from one generation to the next through interaction with neighbors, friends, and family. This is true. But what is it about working-class and middle-class experience that leads to their particular class values? Why, for example, does Tyrec's family value obedience and place a greater emphasis on physical discipline? And why does Alexander's family value self-expression and emphasize discussion, debate, and reasoning? There is no easy answer here, and we must be careful not to overgeneralize from the research findings, but the evidence seems to suggest that cultural capital is closely associated with strategies for success associated with one's job. This makes sense in that one's occupation and work experience are closely associated with one's social class.

In a series of studies conducted across four decades and replicated in several different countries, sociologist Melvin Kohn and his colleagues have found considerable evidence of a relationship between occupation and cultural values.[10] They began their research by classifying jobs in terms of complexity, amount of supervision, and the degree to which required tasks were repetitive or routine. As expected, jobs that are typically considered working class tend to be highly repetitive, not very complex, and closely supervised by a superior. This would be the case, for example, of someone who works on an assembly line at Ford Motor Company, sorts packages on a conveyer belt at United

Parcel Service, or fills fast-food orders for McDonald's. In each case, a supervisor is always close by, the job requires very little training or skill, and the assigned tasks are predictable and monotonous with very little change from day to day. Kohn's research consistently shows that people who work jobs of this type tend to value obedience and conformity to rules.

In contrast, occupations that involve more complex tasks, are free of immediate supervision, and require creative problem solving tend to be jobs associated with the middle and upper-middle class. Think, for example, of someone who works as a political lobbyist for Ford Motor Company, conducts marketing research for the McDonald's Corporation, or is in charge of international finance for United Parcel Service. Consistent with Kohn's expectations, people who work in these occupations tend to place a much higher value on self-direction, initiative, and independence.

Why is this? Why do people in working-class jobs value conformity and obedience, while people in middle-class occupations place a higher value on self-direction and independence? Some might argue that our values affect the jobs that we choose. In other words, people who like boring work and enjoy following rules seek out working-class jobs. This is a plausible explanation. To the extent that the job market is completely free and open and our value system is fixed and unchanging, we might expect people to search for work consistent with their personal values. But the evidence for this causal direction is not strong. Besides, we know that the labor market is not completely free and open and our values are not carved in stone. Therefore, the more compelling explanation is that our values are shaped by our work experience.

Many working-class people quickly learn that initiative, self-direction, and creativity in the workplace will not be rewarded. Someone working an assembly line that deviates from the strictly monitored protocol will be penalized. For the same reason, a package sorter who attempts a creative restructuring of the sorting process will be reprimanded. And someone working a fast-food counter who initiates a new menu item or customer-service strategy could lose his or her job. For working-class employees, "success" on the job is defined in terms of obedience to authority and conformity to a set of formal tasks. Showing up on time and doing as you are told are qualities of a "good worker." Employees in working-class jobs also learn that their feelings or opinions don't matter. Raising concerns about working conditions or complaining about an ineffective supervisor will be interpreted as signs of a "whiner" or "troublemaker."

Contrast the working conditions and performance expectations of a working-class job with those that are found in most upper-middle-class occupations. An attorney, lobbyist, business owner, or top-level manager for a major corporation is expected to be a creative problem solver. Jobs of this type are far from routine, and as a consequence, self-direction and individual initiative are required and rewarded. A quiet and obedient lobbyist who accepted the status quo would be a failure, and a vice president for marketing who did not constantly attempt to explore creative strategies would be fired. In these professional positions, workers learn that their opinion matters and that being assertive and argumentative are valuable attributes.

Parents tend to pass on their values to their children. This is a rather obvious statement. But the research by Kohn and others has shown that some parental values are learned and reinforced in the workplace. This is a significant finding because it helps explain how social class position passes from one generation to the next through the accumulation of different types of cultural capital. When Alexander's parents encourage equal status conversation with adults and use reasoning and logic in their discipline strategy, they are passing on values that are consistent with their professional careers. They know that these skills are central to "success in life"—or at least the upper-middle-class life they are leading. Similarly, when Tyrec's parents stress respect for adults and discipline with direct commands or even a "beating," they too are passing on values and life skills that are critical for success in their world—the working-class world. As a child, Alexander might seem "spoiled" or "demanding," but he is being prepared for a world in which he will be able to command greater deference and respect. Similarly, the fact that Tyrec might have a more restricted vocabulary, less exposure to the arts, and limited contact with upper-class adults will not be seen as a detriment from the perspective of a working-class employer.

THE PRIVILEGE OF CLASS

> She got her good looks from her father. He's a plastic surgeon.
> —Groucho Marx

Children don't select either their parents or their family's social class position; both are "socially inherited." Being born into a wealthy family provides access to economic capital and all of the material advantages associated with having more money. Children in upper-class families are more likely to attend private schools with smaller class sizes. They will live in safer neighborhoods and have easy and regular access to superior nutrition and health care. Private music lessons, educational summer camps, and elite sport teams will be a regular part of their childhood. Acceptance at a top university will seem natural and expected. The cost of tuition will not be a factor. Because summer employment or part-time work will not be necessary, upper-class students will have more time for international travel and professional internships. If they make a youthful mistake and get into trouble with the law, they will have the assistance of an experienced team of lawyers and favors from friends in power. Family connections and friendships developed in college will be an important resource for getting a job, while family trust funds and financial inheritance will help kick-start business ventures and investment portfolios.

Beyond the material advantages associated with economic capital lies a more secret dimension of privilege associated with the inheritance of cultural capital. This is where symbols of status and prestige are passed on from one generation to the next. Most of us glimpse the power of cultural capital while in grade school or high school. Certain kids are "cool" or "hot" while others are "nerds" or "dorks." This is what Nick Bromell discovered when he was ten years old and his parents sent him off to an elite boarding school in New England that catered to young boys from wealthy families:

> Everything revolved around the single principle of status, which was finely elaborated through grades, sports, shoes, shirts, and even socks. Each and every blazer-clad boy knew his place on the status ladder, strove to rise a rung, or dreaded sliding down. At the top were the boys who had everything that counted: family money, athletic ability, and WASPy good looks. Beneath them stood boys with any one of these gifts. [11]

Bromell learned early that even among the most privileged children in a society there is a pecking order that matters. It would be one thing if value associated with clothes, looks, religion, and ethnicity mattered only in grade school and among kids. If this were the case, we could dismiss such a status system as normal, immature, and generally irrelevant to adult success. But in fact, we know that the "value" associated with different forms of cultural capital is a significant factor in the transmission of economic capital and a powerful force in the reproduction of a class system.

There is no denying the rewards that come with individual persistence, effort, and hard work. But individual perseverance alone cannot explain the existence of social classes. Nor can it explain the continuation of class position from one generation to the next. We live our entire lives deeply embedded in a complex web of social connections where economic and cultural forces advantage some and disadvantage others. And as we will see in the following chapter, the extent of our social relationships now reaches well beyond our family and neighborhood to include a historically unprecedented network of global connections.

Chapter Five

Globalization

The Power of Capitalism

> Globalization is not merely a geographic phenomenon which is tearing down national barriers to capital. Globalization is also tearing down ethical and ecological limits on commerce. As everything becomes tradable, everything is for sale. . . . Life has lost its sanctity.
>
> —Vandana Shiva [1]

Tim Dewey is a stout, self-sufficient navy veteran in his midforties. [2] He has little hair on his head and a thick goatee on his chin. Personal responsibility and hard work are important principles for Tim, and he tries to model these values for his teenage son and daughter. Although he is not one to whine or blame others when things go bad, the middle-aged family man felt betrayed when he was first laid off from his job as an aircraft mechanic at United Airlines. After all, Tim reasoned, he was a committed employee who had made sacrifices for the company, and after years of loyal service to United, he was dismissed for "business reasons."

Unemployment was tough and lasted longer than expected. It was twenty-two months before Tim was eventually called back to his old job repairing engines on United's passenger planes. Airline mechanics are among the most skilled and best-paid blue-collar workers in the country, and in 1997 Tim was making $31 an hour. Still, the cost of living in San Francisco was high, and when the opportunity to transfer to the United Airlines maintenance facility in Indianapolis arose, Tim and his wife, Kelly, moved the family to Indiana. Kelly took a job at Lowe's for $10.75 an hour, and between the two of them the family income would be enough to support a comfortable middle-class lifestyle, with full health insurance and enough savings to help out with college tuition for the kids. They were back on track, moving forward toward the American Dream—or so they thought. The experience of economic security turned out to be an illusion.

In 2001, the United Airlines Corporation decided to "outsource" much of its maintenance. Thus, rather than hiring their own mechanics to service the jetliners, they would now contract with a second company to do the work. Because the subcontracting company paid their employees a much lower wage, United could realize significant cost savings. It was a win-win situation for the two businesses, but it was a devastating loss for Tim Dewey and the other mechanics whose jobs were eliminated. Skill, education, and a solid work record were not enough to guarantee job security. With the second layoff Tim came to the brutal realization that he was disposable; the company cared little about his life, and he was not going to let United Airlines control his future anymore: "After the first layoff, I waited desperately for my job to come back; I was not going to wait again."

Drawing on his navy experience and personal values of persistence and independence, Tim decided to start his own business. For almost a year he had had his eye on a water taxi company in Florida. He met the owner while on vacation the previous summer, and the idea of living in a resort town, making a living by shuttling tourists around a lakeshore, was a dream opportunity. As Tim put it, "If I can work the water taxi and never work for anyone again, I'll die a happy man." So the family borrowed $54,000 and purchased an old tour boat from the retiring owner. The plan was for Tim to move to Florida and establish the business ahead of the family. Once the school year was over, Kelly and the kids would follow. But the dream never materialized.

Despite working twelve-hour days, Tim could not attract enough customers to make a decent profit. The summer tourist season was wetter than usual, and the boat needed substantial repairs. By the time his family joined him in Florida, Tim had to admit that his short-lived career as a businessman was a failure. The family could not risk going into any more debt. The Deweys cut their losses, put the boat up for sale, and returned to Indianapolis. In the short term, Kelly's job at Lowe's and Tim's limited unemployment checks would have to sustain the family. In the long term, Tim knew that he would need to learn another job skill, one that could provide hope for a more promising economic future. Securing a career in the expanding computer industry became his new goal.

On the advice of a friend who had also been laid off by United, Tim took advantage of a federally funded retraining program and enrolled in a course of study that would lead to certification as a computer technician. With the certificate in hand, Tim was optimistic that he was on the first step of a promising new path toward economic security. He might have to start out at the bottom, but he was confident in his ability to compete and quickly advance in his new career: "I know several people involved in this and two of them do it as consultants; they have their own little business."

Within twenty-four hours of posting his résumé on the Internet, Tim had a job offer from Bell Tech, a company that provides computer hardware and software services. It wasn't ideal; Tim would be working in their call center, answering phones all day, and the pay was meager, only $12 an hour. But Tim figured he could take more classes, impress his bosses, and improve his wage: "There are huge upside opportunities to grow with this company. . . . Before I leave here I will be doing network administration." His plan was to volunteer extra time for the corporation, introduce himself to upper management, and demonstrate his value as an employee.

But after nine months with Bell Tech, Tim was once again forced to confront a tough economic reality—a significant boost in pay was unlikely. With their oldest son getting ready for college, the Deweys needed to improve the family income fairly soon, so Tim signed up with a temp agency and waited to see if his skills could secure a better-paying job. His wait was short; a local company was looking for experienced airplane mechanics to serve as temporary replacement workers. But in a cruel and ironic twist, Tim was assigned to work at the very same United Airlines maintenance facility from which he had been laid off. Only now he was a temporary worker, employed by the subcontracting company on an impermanent basis. And while his wage of $18 an hour was an improvement over Bell Tech, it didn't come close to the $31 an hour that he had earned doing the same work in the same building several years earlier.

A NEW TYPE OF CAPITALISM

The story of Tim Dewey is not unique. His experience in the job market is similar to that of hundreds of thousands of other U.S. workers who have seen their economic security disrupted over the past thirty years. Indeed, over the past ten years, massive company layoffs have come to be expected. Eastman Kodak cut more than twenty thousand jobs in 1997; Hewlett Packard laid off more than twenty-five thousand in 2001; Verizon eliminated twenty-five thousand positions in 2003; IBM abolished thirteen thousand jobs in 2005; and Bank of America cut sixteen thousand jobs in 2012. The American auto industry has been particularly unstable, with General Motors cutting over thirty thousand jobs between 2005 and 2007, and Ford Motor Company slashing more than seventy thousand jobs between 2002 and 2007. According to one estimate, at least thirty million full-time workers have lost their jobs since the 1980s.[3] While most of these layoffs did not lead to permanent unemployment, they did contribute to the growing ranks of the "downwardly mobile"—workers who are forced into new jobs that pay less, have fewer benefits, and are less secure. If you are presently a college-age student or new to the job market, Tim Dewey's story might seem normal—even expected. But the financial insecurity, job migration, and declining wage experience of the Dewey family reflects a relatively new development in the American economy.

Capitalism is an inherently unstable economic system, but for almost one hundred years, most Americans could expect to benefit economically from an expanding economy. Despite the intermittent ups and downs of the business cycle, sporadic war disruptions, and periodic episodes of economic depression and recession, business success usually translated into greater security, better wages, and improved opportunities for the average working man or woman in the United States. Workers were able to organize strong labor unions to balance the power of big business and provide a voice for their interests. Companies for their part were generally committed to their host communities and typically took pride in maintaining a loyal and steady workforce. While working-class families were never rich, they could expect a stable job in the steel and lumber mills, auto assembly lines, or coal mines that fueled the escalating industrial economy. Economic security was particularly sustained in the decades following World War II. With a high school diploma it was possible to support a family by working for a company that manufactured cameras, sewing machines, furniture, or any of the other products demanded by the growing ranks of optimistic consumers. Self-starting entrepreneurs with a nest egg of savings had a solid chance of success if they opened their own small grocery store, neighborhood laundry, or family restaurant. Perhaps most importantly, it was a reasonable and likely expectation for children to be better off economically than their parents.

This relatively stable and more or less predictable form of capitalism has all but disappeared. In its place is a "new capitalism," one that is less committed to local communities, more global in its scope and orientation, and brutal in its effect on the psyche of the worker. Before 1980, one could assume that increased productivity and growing profit would translate into better wages for employees. However, over the last quarter of a century, the U.S. gross domestic product rose by almost two-thirds while the inflation-adjusted wage for the average worker involved in manufacturing actually fell. In other words, U.S. workers are still producing enormous amounts of wealth for their companies, but they are receiving a much smaller share of it in return. Men like Tim Dewey, who have a high school education and blue-collar job skills, are having their lives disrupted and their work identities challenged by corporations that are now more concerned with a rapid return on recent investments than the long, steady, and predictable growth of a company. What might be good for a large multinational business or wealthy investor in the short term is disturbing the steady, stable, and predictable life of families and their communities.

This became shockingly obvious in 2008 when the global economy experienced its biggest catastrophe since the Great Depression. In a sudden and disastrous sequence of events, major banks in the United States and Europe collapsed, and the stock value of major corporations plummeted by an average of 20 percent in six weeks—along with the retirement investments of millions of people. Home values were cut almost in half, and the massive number of foreclosures left some neighborhoods in the United States looking like ghost towns. Between January 2008 and June 2009 over eight million jobs were lost as the unemployment rate went from 4.8 percent to 10 percent in a matter of months.

There are a many factors that contributed to this crisis, but economist Joseph Stiglitz, a Nobel Prize winner, expertly summarized the essential cause of the "great recession" when he said, "The major lesson of this crisis is that the pursuit of self-interest, particularly within the financial sector, may not lead to societal well-being, unless we set the rules of the games correctly. Fixing these 'rules of the game' is the big task ahead."[4] Indeed, but unfortunately, the current rules of the new capitalism have not yet been changed, and the vast majority of people continue to suffer as a consequence.

In the United States today the fastest-growing segment of the labor force is temporary work. Companies such as Manpower U.S., Labor Ready, and Office Team are becoming an increasingly dominant part of the economy as they serve to place new and unemployed workers in temporary and part-time jobs. As Tim Dewey discovered, temporary work is low paying and does not come with health insurance or retirement benefits. In 1970 the largest employer in the United States was General Motors, a flourishing automobile producer whose workers could expect to retire after thirty years of work with full health benefits for the entire family. Experienced line workers at General Motors could earn as much as $30 an hour and leave with an annual pension at retirement of $30,000. At its peak, GM employed more than six hundred thousand Americans in blue-collar jobs; but today the number is down to around one hundred thousand. The downsizing of General Motors' American workforce is mirrored in other working-class production jobs. As a consequence, large manufacturing companies no longer provide the most jobs in America. In 2012, the largest U.S. employer was Wal-Mart, where the average wage is less than $11 an hour and most employees work less than forty hours a week. The second largest U.S. employer is the McDonald's fast-food restaurant chain.

American workers struggling to adjust to declining incomes and downward mobility have been trapped by debt and forced into personal bankruptcy. More than one and a half million families filed for bankruptcy in 2010 compared to only 285,000 in 1980. This jump represents a startling increase of over 500 percent in just thirty years, and researchers have estimated that about 60 percent of all bankruptcies in 2007 were caused by unmanageable medical bills.[5] When Tim Dewey's water taxi service failed to turn a profit, he was forced to declare bankruptcy, and shortly thereafter he grew ill and ended up spending six days in the hospital with a heart condition. But because he was a navy veteran, his treatment and care was paid for by the federal government; most Americans are not as fortunate. In 2011 more than forty-eight million citizens of the United Sates had no health insurance.

The negative impact of the new capitalism is wide ranging and has consequences that reach down deep to core issues of self and identity.

When workers are laid off, have their salary reduced, or struggle to find steady work, they often attribute their poor economic plight to personal failings or limitations. This is a feature of American individualism. In a culture that puts a heavy emphasis on personal agency and independent effort, it can be difficult to recognize or acknowledge the controlling influence of large social processes. But the life trajectory of Tim Dewey and the millions of other families who share his story is in fact being shaped by powerful forces of a new global capitalism. It is a new capitalism that uproots families who must migrate to find better work. It is a new capitalism that limits full-time employment to shorter periods with multiple companies, and it is new capitalism that leaves workers and their families with an increased sense of insecurity and anxiety.

Sociologist Richard Sennett, who has conducted several studies of the cultural impact of recent economic changes, has summarized the corrosive character of the new capitalism:

> How can long-term purposes be pursued in a short-term society? How can durable social relationships be sustained? How can a human being develop a narrative of identity and life history in a society composed of episodes and fragments? The conditions of the new economy feed instead on experience which drifts in time, from place to place, from job to job . . . short-term capitalism threatens to corrode . . . character, particularly those qualities of character which bind human beings to one another and furnishes each with a sense of sustainable self.[6]

All of us need a sustainable sense of self, a feeling of purpose and meaning, a reason to get out of bed in the morning, to believe that our life matters, that we are needed, and that we make a difference somehow in the world. As we saw in chapter 2, human beings are first, foremost, and fundamentally social animals. Our identities are products of social relationships, and when predictable social connections are disrupted, we feel alienated, lost, dejected, and depressed. Most of us recognize this psychological state in the grief we experience following the death of a loved one. But it is also associated with the loss of any steady or long-term relationships—the breakup of a marriage, a child moving away, the termination of a friendship, or the retirement of a colleague. This is why a job loss can be so devastating. To be laid off from a job means much more than simply losing a paycheck—it can also be an overwhelming blow to one's social identity and sense of self. Unemployed workers are more likely to suffer from depression, alcohol abuse, and an assortment of physical ailments.[7] In extreme cases it can even lead to suicide. In fact, research demonstrates that the risk of suicide is up to three times higher among those who are unemployed.[8]

The instability and uncertainty associated with unemployment sends out shock waves that can weaken and overturn other social relationships. As one might expect, marriages suffer when a spouse is laid off. The financial challenges, personal depression, and general frustration associated with job loss will substantially increase the likelihood of divorce. Moreover, there is strong evidence indicating that job instability also reduces the likelihood of getting married in the first place.[9] Steady and predictable relationships in one part of our lives depend upon steady and predictable relationships in other parts. The networks of social connections that define a community are like strings of an interwoven fabric; pulling on one can lead to the unraveling of an entire garment. We can see evidence of this domino effect most clearly in the devastating social consequences that result when a small- or medium-sized city loses a major employer.

COMMUNITIES IN CRISIS

Lorain, Ohio, is typical of many towns in the so-called industrial belt of the upper Midwest of the United States. It was founded in the early 1800s on the shore of Lake Erie and grew to a population of over seventy thousand by the end of the twentieth century. The shipbuilding companies, steel mills, and auto industry provided generations of residents with stable jobs that sustained the thriving community. But sometime in the 1980s, the local economy began to unravel as corporations started to "outsource," "subcontract," "merge," and "restructure" in search of greater profits. In 1982, U.S. Steel laid off 1,800 workers in Lorain. Ford Motor Company was not far behind; it eliminated several production lines at the Lorain plant and shipped hundreds of auto-assembly jobs to factories in Mexico where worker wages and benefits were much lower. The slow exodus of manufacturing jobs continued for two decades, and the reverberations were felt in other industries. In 2001, Marconi Communications "reorganized" its company and laid off 425 employees in Lorain. The city estimated that it lost $500,000 annually in tax income from the Marconi layoffs alone. In 2002, Republic Engineered Products, a spin-off of U.S. Steel, laid off another 300 workers and cut employee pay by 15 percent. In 2004, Ford shut down the entire Lorain plant, a devastating blow that resulted in 1,700 lost jobs and cut income tax revenue by approximately $2.4 million. The following year, Century Telephone dismissed several hundred workers, and Federated Department Stores cut 95 computer operations jobs at its Lorain facility. When the economic foundation of a town begins to crumble, the link between stable, well-paying jobs and overall community health is made visible.

Between 1995 and 2005, delinquent property taxes more than doubled in the city while government debt skyrocketed. With declining revenues, the Lorain municipal government was forced to lay off workers, only adding to the growing ranks of the unemployed. As a consequence, potholes in the streets went unfilled, grass in the city parks became overgrown, and parts of downtown looked abandoned. Storefronts that used to house furniture stores, clothing boutiques, beauty salons, hardware shops, and florists emptied and were boarded up.[10] With fewer dollars circulating in the local economy, small businesses and nonprofit civic groups also suffer. Little League baseball teams struggle to find sponsors, local churches have had to cut back on services, and a Catholic high school was forced to close down. In 2007, the Lorain public school district, the third-largest employer in the city, cut its staff by one-third, resulting in layoff notices being sent to 250 school teachers.

Unfortunately, the experience of Lorain, Ohio, is not unique. When high-wage working-class jobs leave town, the economic reverberations have wide-ranging social consequences. This is especially true in the inner city of many urban centers where the new economy has failed to create sustainable jobs for more than a generation. As a consequence, criminal behavior can become the only predictable source of income. When the legitimate economy cannot provide jobs or a promising future for young people, illegal black market economies offer underground alternatives for psychological escape and a quick infusion of cash. Sociologist Elijah Anderson, who has conducted in-depth analyses of the life experiences of young people in poor inner-city neighborhoods, summarizes the issue well:

> The economic unraveling in so many of these communities puts people up against the wall and encourages them to do things that they would otherwise be morally reluctant to do. A boy who can't get a job in the regular economy becomes a drug dealer not all at once but by increments. These boys make a whole lot of choices and decisions based in part on what they are able to do successfully. A boy who grows up on the streets thoroughly invested in the code of the street is also closer to

the underground economy. Once mastered, the savoir faire of the street world—knowing how to deal coolly with people, how to move, look, act, dress—is a form of capital, not a form middle-class people would respect, but capital that can nonetheless be cashed in. [11]

Violence is also an undesirable by-product of a downwardly spiraling economy. The illegal drug trade is especially dangerous in that it is sanctioned and controlled by physical force and threats of violence. Analyses of crime statistics show that cities that have suffered the most from plant closings and downsizing experience significant increases in homicide. [12] With growing rates of crime and violence and neighborhoods falling into disrepair, large corporate employers have an additional excuse to leave town, and customers that would normally patronize neighborhood shops have another reason to stay away.

It is a cycle of inequality that hits the poorest and most vulnerable citizens the hardest. In 1975, just before the new capitalism began to take hold, there were less than four hundred thousand Americans behind bars, but by 2010, the number had skyrocketed to 2.2 million—an increase of more than 500 percent! The United States now has the highest rate of incarceration in the world. The majority of the new prisoners come from poor neighborhoods and have extensive histories of unemployment. Moreover, our justice system is not color blind. African Americans, for example, who have been exploited by slavery, segregation, and racist government policies for centuries, are particularly vulnerable to economic decline. The unemployment rate for young African American men is more than twice the rate for young white men. One consequence of economic inequality is exploitation in the criminal justice system. The percentage of young African American men in prison is nearly seven times that of white men, and while African American men make up only 14 percent of the population of men in the United States, they represent over 40 percent of the prison population. [13]

In a desperate attempt to recover from the ravages of the new economy, many towns have looked to the expanding prison industry in an effort to secure stable employment for its citizens. The sad irony of course is that the economic forces responsible for plant closings and unemployment have also contributed to the social conditions associated with criminal behavior, which in turn have spurred the public policy support for building more prisons! Like a gambler who "doubles up" after every loss, community leaders and politicians are often sucked into a spiraling descent of false hope. When governments direct dwindling tax dollars to prison construction, other social service needs suffer. In the decades between 1980 and 2000, the share of state and local tax dollars spent on prisons grew by 104 percent, while the relative share of spending on higher education dropped by 21 percent. Today, the state of California spends as much money incarcerating prisoners as it does educating its public university students. In Illinois there are nearly twenty thousand more African Americans in the state's prison system than in the state's colleges and universities. With more tax dollars diverted to correctional institutions, the cost of a public university education has also increased as students are asked to share a greater percentage of the educational load. Tuition at public universities has increased substantially, while at the same time financial aid in the form of grants has declined. My own state of Oregon is typical. In 1986 the average cost of tuition and fees was about $1,500 a year. By 2012, the cost had increased to $8,000 annually. Even after adjusting for inflation, this represents a doubling of the cost for tuition alone. When the costs of textbooks and living expenses are added to the mix, a four-year college education at a public university will cost about $21,000 a year. This is clearly a barrier to many families. The end result is that access to a college education is immensely more challenging today than it was twenty-five years ago.[14]

One cannot look at the issues of unemployment, crime, divorce, lack of education, and poor health and conclude that it simply reflects individual limitations or personal weakness. Individual troubles, such as those experienced by Tim Dewey and his family, are part of a much larger pattern of social problems. A radically individualist approach to social problems ignores the power of social forces that have worked to produce a legacy of injustice and inequality. Tim Dewey may not understand that his emotional roller coaster and financial free fall is the result of large-scale shifts in economic forces outside of his individual control. Nevertheless, there is little doubt that the new capitalism is eroding the foundation of social life for the Deweys and other American families. And as we shall see in the next section, the life-changing power of the new capitalism is not limited to the United States but has a reach that extends around the globe.

CHINA BLUES

Jasmine sits at a table surrounded on three sides by stacks of recently sewn designer blue jeans. Her silky, black hair is tied in a long ponytail that hangs down to the middle of her back. Her shoulders are slumped, and she appears to be on the verge of tears. A stern factory supervisor hovers over her left shoulder, demanding that she pick up the pace. In her hand Jasmine fumbles a small pair of scissors that she uses to cut the loose threads on the jeans. [15]

Although Jasmine recently turned sixteen, she looks much younger. She is petite, just barely over five feet tall, and has a round, soft face with dark eyes. On this day she has been working for seventeen hours to meet a production deadline. She is not alone; there are more than seven hundred other workers at the plant, and most are teenage girls; many are as young as fourteen. The factory production floor is a drab cement room that looks like a parking garage with long columns of hanging fluorescent lights. Rows of work tables are cluttered with garments in various stages of assembly. The girls work at a frantic pace, sewing, cutting, folding, and packaging. They are not allowed to speak to each other. Video cameras monitor the shop floor, and a large poster on the factory wall reads, "If you don't work hard today you'll look hard for work tomorrow!"

This is not the life Jasmine expected to find when she left her rural village in the Sichuan Province of central China. For generations her family survived by raising goats and ducks, and by growing rice on terraced slopes. But politics and the economy changed, and Jasmine understood that her family needed her to find factory work in one of the new industrial cities on the east coast. Like many other young people in her village, she took a two-day train trip to the city of Guangzhou, a bustling industrial city of over five million people on the Pearl River Delta in southeast China. She had a one-way ticket and one hundred yuan—about twelve U.S. dollars—that her father had saved for her trip. It was her first time on a train and her first trip to a city.

The Lifeng Clothes Company where Jasmine works is typical of many garment factories in this industrial region of China. It is a stark four-story building with cement walls surrounded by a steel fence. The entrance to the compound is monitored by a young but stern-looking security guard who checks for proper identification and searches the bags of all employees before they exit the grounds. Most workers, however, rarely have time to leave. They work long hours, seven days a week, and they are housed and fed in a bleak dormitory inside the factory gates. Jasmine's bed is crammed into a room she shares with eleven other girls. The heating is poor, and in the winter she must wear her clothes to bed in an effort to stay warm. For all of this she will earn less than $2 a day. The company will deduct food and housing expenses and will charge extra for a bucket of warm water that she will use to wash her clothes. If Jasmine is late to work in the morning she will be fined; if she gets sick or pregnant she will be fired. She misses her family but can't afford the trip home. A train ticket is equivalent to one month's salary, and she has not been working long enough to save for the trip. "I wish I could go home but my family will be disappointed," she laments. "I'd be ashamed. I can't let them down. They are really counting on me."

While Jasmine's life may be bleak, the owner of the Lifeng factory, Mr. Lam, is doing quite well. The former police chief oversees a staff of managers from a large modern office. He drives a late model Mercedes Benz and negotiates business contracts over dinner in expensive restaurants with distributors from France, Australia, England, Canada, and the United States. He shows little concern for his employees and does not believe that they are being exploited; if anything, Mr. Lam feels like he is the victim: "The workers take advantage of us," he complains. "When they work overtime we give them a free snack at midnight." Like many employers in China, Mr. Lam prefers to hire young girls from rural villages because they are more compliant and less likely to resist the demanding work schedule. Still, he is suspicious and unsatisfied with his workers' attitude. In his words, "migrant workers only want to feather their own nest. Many violate the law. When they see other people's nice things they get jealous."

Jasmine, however, has no material ambitions; her only consuming desire is to return home: "If my mom were here I would run into her arms and cry my eyes out. Maybe this is just a bad dream. When I wake up I will be back at school playing with friends."

GLOBAL CONNECTIONS

Although Jasmine's heartrending story may seem unrelated to Tim Dewey's struggle to find a stable, family-wage job, the turbulence experienced in both lives is in fact a product of "globalization." The economic forces that propelled Jasmine to leave her rural village for factory work in the city are the same forces that induced Tim to move his family from California to Indiana to Florida and back again to Indiana. The new economic conditions pressing against both Jasmine and Tim are part of a global capitalism that operates with unprecedented speed and scope. While East Asian countries such as China have been trading with Europe and North America for hundreds of years, it was never as extensive and as immediately consequential for so many people as it is today. In the late eighteenth century, a trade ship leaving New York harbor with a cargo of animal skins for Chinese merchants would return with a shipment of tea, silk, and spice for American consumers. The entire economic exchange, including travel and time spent negotiating with merchants, would take more than a year to complete. Today, million-dollar deals can be completed electronically in a matter of hours, and products from China can reach U.S. shipping ports in a matter of days. In the 1850s, when California industrialists needed a cheap source of labor to work the mines and build the railroads, they recruited Chinese immigrants to work for minimal wages under exploitive conditions. Today many U.S. industrialists seeking the same source of cheap labor have simply moved their production facilities to China or have subcontracted with a Chinese company. As large multinational corporations sprint around the world in search of quicker and larger profit, concerns of the average laborer are pushed aside and dismissed as an unfortunate but necessary adjustment to a new business model.

"Globalization" is the term that sociologists and others use to describe the dramatic economic and cultural changes that characterize the new capitalism. We can define "globalization" in neutral terms as the increasing cross-border flows of goods, services, money, people, information, and culture leading to greater economic and political interdependence. Defined in this way, globalization sounds quite positive. Indeed, for some politicians, economists, and social commentators, globalization is an inevitable evolutionary development that will eventually bring economic and social progress to the world. For this reason, U.S. presidents from Ronald Reagan to Barack Obama have been cheerleaders for globalization and the new global marketplace that it promises. Large corporations and international finance organizations such as the World Bank argue that "free trade" between countries will reduce global poverty and improve social development. The problem with this optimistic view, however, is that it selectively ignores the fact that globalization in its present form is not an open, free, and democratic process. A small number of powerful institutions and wealthy individuals have more control over the shape and direction of the globalization process than the millions of workers whose livelihood is at stake. As a consequence, the "interdependence" that is being created is not one of equality or hope for most people in the world. Multinational corporations are certainly benefiting from globalization, but workers are for the most part suffering.

Jasmine's monotonous task of trimming threads on a pair of jeans is a small link in an incredibly large production chain. When a typical American consumer purchases a pair of pants at Wal-Mart or a new shirt at Nordstrom, he or she is most likely unaware of the toil that Jasmine and her coworkers have endured. And when Jasmine and other Chinese workers migrate to apparel factories in the city, they are oblivious to the fact that U.S. men and women lost their livelihood when their company moved production to China. Between 1997 and 2009, 649 factories in the U.S. textile and apparel industry have been shut down as companies such as Fruit of the Loom and Burlington Industries shifted production overseas to countries such as El Salvador, Vietnam, and China. In the five-year period between 2002 and 2007, over three hundred thousand U.S. workers who produced linens, towels, clothing, yarn, and fabrics have seen their jobs disappear.[16] Most textile production in the United States occurs in small- to medium-sized towns in the Southeast where the average wage in the apparel industry is less than $500 a week. But even with wages of less than $10 an hour, it is impossible for U.S. workers to compete with laborers who earn significantly less than $1 an hour in countries thousands of miles away.

At its peak, the Fruit of the Loom factory in Campbellsville, Kentucky, had more than four thousand employees. Nearly 40 percent of the town worked at the factory, and everyone seemed to have a family connection with the company. Mothers and fathers, brothers and sisters, and aunts and uncles all earned a living making T-shirts and briefs for the same small-town employer. Many employees had spent more than twenty years working for Fruit of the Loom; a few had worked at the same plant for four decades, and it was hard to imagine Campbellsville without Fruit of the Loom. But in June 1998, corporate executives decided to close the Campbellsville plant and open a new factory in El Salvador. When the decision was announced over the factory loudspeaker, most employees were stunned; some broke down and cried uncontrollably.

In its new Central American location, Fruit of the Loom would eventually employ about eight thousand Salvadorans in factory jobs that paid between $5 and $10 a day for nine to ten hours of work. Maria Quiroa was a typical employee. She earned about $50 a week packing boxes at the end of the production line. It was monotonous work, but the thirty-year-old single mother was hopeful that her new job would provide financial security and a stable life for her family. But like the Fruit of the Loom employees in Campbellsville, Kentucky, Maria did not anticipate the callous and calculated speed of the new economy. In 2004, she was laid off along with five hundred other employees when the company decided to shift production to China. Unemployed and desperate, Maria decided to attempt a risky migration to the United States where she hoped to find work that would pay enough to allow her to send money home to relatives who would be caring for her son. Even though her journey would be fraught with danger and would require three illegal border crossings, Maria had few other options and decided to make the trip. The plan, however, was at least temporarily derailed after she was apprehended at the Guatemala-Mexico border and sent home.[17]

So why is China fast becoming the preferred destination for large manufacturing companies? With the ease of global communication and the speed of modern transportation, geographic distance is no longer a barrier for companies headquartered in North America or Europe. Besides, China can offer corporations a more desirable "business climate." This is a euphemistic reference to the fact that the Chinese government can guarantee very low wages, long workdays, minimal business taxes, and few health, safety, and environmental restrictions. There are millions of workers like Jasmine in thousands of new factories in the most populous nation on earth, available for exploitation and waiting to improve the profit margin of a foreign company. The fact that China has a suspect record of democracy and outlaws independent labor unions is irrelevant to most businesses. In fact, for many potential investors this is simply another indicator of a healthy business climate. All that matters is that China remains committed to capitalism.

With more than $1 billion from foreign investors pouring into the country every week, China is experiencing an unprecedented social transformation. New industrial cities are springing up in a matter of a few years, and established urban centers are expanding at record pace, along with the attendant problems of air and water pollution, overcrowding, and crime. The city of Shenzhen, for example, was an average-sized city in the 1980s with a total population of 310,000. However, its location in the industrial region of the Pearl River Delta made it a prime target for economic development and foreign capital investment. After the Chinese government designated the region a "special economic zone," the city population ballooned to 3.45 million by 1995, and over the next ten years it added another six million residents. Today Shenzhen has a population of over ten million and is still growing at a startling rate. What is particularly striking about this growth is that almost all of the newcomers are considered by the Chinese government to be "temporary residents" and are not recognized as official citizens of the city. As a consequence their political power is considerably limited. Most are young female immigrants like Jasmine who leave rural villages in the west in search of economic success only to find temporary factory employment under harsh conditions.[18]

It is important to recognize that the flight of capital and jobs from the United States to Asia is not limited to the apparel industry or to the blue-collar manufacturing sector. In fact, of the top 500 largest corporations in the world, 450 of them have substantial business investments in China. Companies in the computer industry and other high-tech fields are also finding ways to take advantage of the low wages and reduced benefits of workers in other countries. In 2006, for example, Intel, the world's largest producer of computer chips, announced that it was cutting 10,500 jobs in the United States while investing $1 billion to dramatically expand its chip-assembly and testing plant in Vietnam. In 2005, IBM, the largest information technology company in the world, decided to lay off thirteen thousand workers in the United States and Europe and hire more than fourteen thousand new employees in India. In the United States, an experienced software programmer will earn between $75,000 and $80,000 a year, but an equally skilled programmer in India will make somewhere between $15,000 to $20,000 annually. For this reason, it is no surprise that IBM had 73,000 employees in India in 2007 with plans to add many more workers in the future.

Tim Dewey learned through experience that the computer industry in the United States is not a field with expanding opportunities. The number of computer hardware jobs has actually declined since the year 2000, and the total number of software jobs in the United States has flattened out over the same period. The entry-level positions in call centers where Tim Dewey started out have particularly high turnover rates and are also easy targets for outsourcing to foreign countries. In India, a typical call-center employee with a college education and excellent English skills will earn less than $200 a month. With this type of global competition, it is not surprising that Tim Dewey's prospects for a wage increase at Bell Tech were relatively limited.

WHO BENEFITS?

There is no disputing the fact that global capitalism is producing new and expanding sources of wealth. In 2012 there were 1,226 people in the world with a net worth of over $1 billion dollars. In the United States alone there are now 425 billionaires, up from only 13 in 1982. More importantly, this growth trend is not limited to the wealthy countries of North America, Europe, and Japan. Countries such as China, India, and Mexico now have their share of the super rich. According to a 2012 report in *Forbes* magazine, there are 48 billionaires in India and 95 billionaires in China, while Mexico is now home to the richest man in the world—Carlos Slim. Mr. Slim, who made his fortune in telecommunications, banking, and consumer electronics, was worth $69 billion dollars in 2012, just slightly ahead of Bill Gates, the cofounder of Microsoft. The enormity of such wealth is difficult for the average person to appreciate. We can, however, get some relative sense of how much money we are talking about by breaking it down into the equivalent of an hourly wage. Take, for example, Phil Knight, the founder of Nike. Between 2006 and 2007, Mr. Knight's net worth increased by over $2 billion. This means that he received more than $2.7 million dollars every day, the equivalent of over $228,000 an hour, for every hour of every day in the year!

While the rich in the world are obviously getting richer at record rates, the poor remain stuck in poverty. Over 1 billion people struggle to survive on less than $1 a day and another 1.2 billion live off of $1 to $2 a day. It is estimated that more than 40 percent of the world's population is currently living under conditions of extreme poverty. Never before in the history of the world have we witnessed such extreme inequality. According to a United Nations Human Development Report, the richest fifty individuals in the world have a combined income that is greater than the combined income of the poorest 416 million people.[19] Not only does the inequality persist between rich and poor nations, but it is also evident within every country. The average American, for example, is 61 times as rich as the average citizen of Tanzania, but in the United States the top 1 percent of families makes over one million dollars a year, while the bottom 90 percent average about $31,000.

As corporations accumulate greater wealth, they are concentrating more of their profit in the pockets of their top managers. Thus, between 1978 and 2011, the average chief executive officer (CEO) in the United States saw pay rise by 725 percent, while the average worker saw wages increase by just 5.7 percent over the same period. The heads of big companies have always made more money than their employees, but the income gap separating the elites in the office from the frontline laborer is growing at a disturbing pace. In 1965, for example, the average CEO earned 24 times more than the average worker, but by 2011 the average CEO pay was 380 times greater than that of the average worker.

With very few exceptions, most of these top executives believe that they deserve every penny of their accumulated fortune. Billionaire banker Sanford I. Weill, for example, has defended the massive concentration of income and wealth in the hands of corporate leaders by saying, "We didn't rely on somebody else to build what we built." Such a statement, however, arrogantly ignores the sweat and toil of workers all over the world whose labor remains the foundation of the new global economy. Adding insult to injury, many chief executives working in the new capitalism are actually rewarded for cutting jobs and reducing wages. The case of John Trani is typical. In 1997, Mr. Trani was hired by the Stanley Corporation with a signing bonus of $1 million and the promise of another $1 million annual salary. Over the next six years he proceeded to close forty-three company factories while cutting more than 5,500 jobs. For his efforts he received an $8 million bonus and an annual retirement pension of $1.3 million. In a similar display of heartless greed, Carly Fiorina, the CEO of Hewlett-Packard in 2001, saw her compensation jump from $1.2 million to $4.1 million after removing more than twenty-five thousand people from the company payroll.

For the most part, the world's super rich and the masses of extremely poor have very little contact with each other. But this does not mean that their lives are not connected. Economic decisions made by men like Phil Knight have enormous consequences for young girls like Jasmine who toil in the apparel industry. And as we shall see in the following section, sometimes the link between the rich and the poor is of a very intimate and personal nature.

ROWENA

Rowena Bautista lives in large brick home in an upscale Washington, D.C., neighborhood. [20] She is a loving mother who rises every morning at 7:00 a.m. to care for two-year-old Noa. After breakfast, Rowena and Noa will spend the day taking walks in the park, reading at the local library, or visiting with playmates. In the afternoon, the two will curl up together for a nap, and Noa will be comforted as Rowena softly coos a children's lullaby. While Rowena and Noa may display the tender affection typical of mother and daughter, Noa is not Rowena's child.

Rowena receives room and board and $750 a month to serve as Noa's live-in nanny. It is a job that Rowena performs with both affection and sorrow. Rowena's own children, nine-year-old Clinton and ten-year-old Princela, live ten thousand miles away in the village of Camiling, Philippines. She left them seven years ago, when they were about the same age as Noa. When Rowena recently received news that her children were ill, her eyes welled up with tears: "I should be with my children when they're sick. That's what a mother does." Instead, Rowena gives her heart to someone else's child. "I give Noa what I can't give my children. She makes me feel like a mother."

Noa's mother, Myra, is grateful for the trusting care provided by Rowena. As a busy executive for an international public relations firm, she does not have the time to look after Noa during the week. The same is true for Noa's father, who works for a foreign embassy. Instead, the ambitious young couple depends on Rowena to nurture their only child. Myra appreciates the help but also recognizes the irony of their relationship: "Rowena's made an incredible sacrifice for her children and I know that. But I can't imagine making that sacrifice with my daughter."

Rowena hasn't been back to the Philippines in over two years, and the physical distance separating Rowena and her children has contributed to an emotional chasm. Clinton and Princela have come to expect gifts in the mail and occasional phone calls but little else. Back in Camiling, Clinton and Princela receive most of their care from Anna de la Cruz, who arrives every morning to cook, clean, and look after Rowena's children. The attachment Anna feels toward Clinton and Princela mirrors the attachment Rowena feels toward baby Noa. In a sad and ironic twist, Rowena sends Anna $50 a month to serve as a nanny to her own children in the Philippines. But Anna is also a mother, and while she is working as a nanny, her son is cared for by Anna's mother-in-law. Thus, through a series of surrogate relationships, Myra, Rowena, Anna, and Anna's mother-in-law are linked in a global "mothering chain" that separates mother and child. It is a heartrending trend that leaves most women and children unsatisfied. Despite the sad consequences, international mothering chains are increasingly common and growing at an unprecedented pace. It is a new family form that is encouraged and sustained by the bizarre logic of global capitalism.

As strange as it may sound, Rowena left her children because she wanted to care for them. Despite three years of college, Rowena was unable to find work that would provide a living wage. By working as a nanny in the United States she can afford to send home $400 a month, an amount greater than what is earned by the doctor in her village. Rowena's husband does not contribute to the family. He moved to South Korea for work, but when Rowena and the children were deported by immigration authorities, the couple lost contact.

Like many rural villages in the Philippines, Camiling is in economic decline. Crime, drug use, and homelessness are widespread. Many homes have no electricity or running water. It is estimated that 30 percent of Filipino children have a parent that has migrated out of the country for work. For Rowena, migration to the United States is a personal, heart-wrenching solution to a very impersonal, global problem.

CARE FOR SALE

The story of Rowena reminds us that globalization is not only about production, trade, and profit. In homes throughout the world, the new global capitalism is also reshaping fundamental human relationships. In one sector of the global economy, laborers might work to produce clothes, food, computers, and cars, but in another sector they are hired to provide housecleaning, cooking, child care, conversation, comfort, and even love. From day care centers to retirement homes, in suburban ranch houses and high-rise apartments, migrant workers are being paid to look after young children, tend to the needs of elderly parents, clean bathrooms, and make dinner. Most of these migrants are from poor countries, and the vast majority of them are women who are engaged in a type of emotional labor in which feeling and sentiment are exchanged for a wage. Like multinational corporations that have "outsourced" production and labor to Asia and Latin America, many upper-middle-class families now "subcontract" for services that have traditionally been provided by relatives.

Sociologist Arlie Russell Hochschild uses the story of Rowena Bautista to illustrate what she calls the "care drain," or the movement of care workers from the impoverished regions of the world to the wealthy regions of the world. The act of migration may be voluntary, but for most people it is a frightening choice made under pressure and in desperation. It is estimated that in 2010 there were forty-two million immigrants living in the United States, both legal and illegal, and about half were women. When poor, young mothers like Rowena leave their children to care for the children of wealthy Americans, the hardship is greatest for the children left behind. They suffer the loss of affection and physical contact that is in effect extracted from one family and transferred to another. In the words of Hochschild, it is a "global heart transplant," and "in the end, both First and Third World women are small players in a larger economic game whose rules they have not written."[21]

Today there are close to two hundred million people who, like Rowena, have moved from their country of birth to another country in search of work. In addition, there are hundreds of millions of others like Tim and Jasmine who have left their hometowns in search of a better life. Not surprisingly, wealthy countries are the most common destination while poor countries are the usual starting place. Mexico, for example, has close to a million out-migrants every year. In Europe, Spain receives over five hundred thousand newcomers while North African countries such as Morocco and Egypt lose over one hundred thousand each.

There is no doubt that we are living in an age of intense migration; and the flow of people across and within national borders is more extensive now than in any other time in human history. So what is the motivation? Why are people leaving their homeland and their families at such an extraordinary rate? While there are many reasons for migration, most people are compelled to move because of economic pressures. Rowena's motivation is typical. She wanted to escape poverty, and she hoped to secure a brighter economic future for her children. The $400 a month that she sends back to the Philippines may not seem like much, but for the Bautista family it is the difference between poverty and security, illness and health, and resignation and hope.

Collectively, money sent by migrants back home to families in developing countries has become a key component in the global economy. Without this infusion of foreign currency many national economies would falter. In 2010, these "remittances" totaled more than $400 billion, and Mexico, China, and India each received over $50 billion from citizens living abroad. This is an enormous infusion of cash that exceeds traditional forms of foreign aide. In the case of the Philippines, it has been estimated that 34 to 54 percent of the population is sustained by money sent home by migrant workers, two-thirds of whom are women. Because most of the Filipina migrants end up working in the care industry as aides in nursing homes, as domestics, or as nannies, one sociologist has concluded about the Philippines that "care is now the country's primary export."[22]

Yet, one of the ironies of the new global economy is that while it is becoming easier for corporations to move from country to country, it is becoming more difficult for individuals to follow the same path. So-called free trade agreements between nations are in effect opening borders for companies like Boeing, Intel, Levi Strauss, and Nike, who have successfully lobbied for new laws that facilitate the free movement of capital. But at the same time, many national governments are now working to limit the legal migration of workers like Rowena Bautista and Maria Quiroa. For centuries, people have moved from country to country with very few legal regulations. But in the present political environment, migration is tightly controlled and is becoming more restrictive. The United States, for example, uses a quota system that puts severe limits on the entry of poor people and gives overwhelming priority to workers who have an "extraordinary ability in the sciences, arts, education, business, or athletics, are outstanding professors or researchers" or who are "foreign nationals that are managers and executives subject to international transfer to the United States."[23] Workers outside of these elite categories have little chance of being accepted. As a consequence, it is estimated that about eleven million U.S. residents are undocumented immigrants, who have either crossed the border illegally or who have decided to live in the country with an expired visa.[24]

Still, the vast majority of current U.S. residents were actually born in America (87 percent), and of those who migrated from another country, most are documented legal residents (71 percent). Moreover, economists agree that the economic impact of migrant labor (both legal and illegal) is overwhelmingly positive in terms of overall wealth production. Nevertheless, there are politicians and activist citizens in the United States and other wealthy countries who argue in favor of greater limits on immigration. Some even believe that the answer lies in constructing thousands of miles of walls as a security barrier. But building higher fences while "cracking down" on "illegals" is an approach that fails to account for the complexity of social connections, both emotional and economic, that serve to sustain and motivate dangerous and agonizing acts of migration. A bigger and better wall will not alter the new global economy, reduce poverty, or curtail economic exploitation; these are social forces that cannot be easily fenced in.

Chapter Six

Violence, Sex, and Politics

The Power of Mass Media

Despite the variety and the differences, and however much we proclaim the contrary, what the media produce is neither spontaneous nor completely "free": "news" does not just happen, pictures and ideas do not merely spring from reality into our eyes and minds, truth is not directly available, we do not have unrestrained variety at our disposal.

—Edward W. Said[1]

A royal scandal engulfed the British monarchy in the summer of 2012 when embarrassing photographs of Prince Harry (son of Prince Charles and Princess Diana, and grandson of Queen Elizabeth II) appeared on the Internet tabloid TMZ and were immediately featured by over one hundred other websites, including global news giants CNN and CBS. The grainy cell phone photos were snapped in a Las Vegas hotel room during a raging party where a game of "strip billiards" left the twenty-seven-year-old prince stark naked. In one photo he is seen standing with his head turned toward a television with his hands discretely cupping what one news tabloid referred to as "the royal jewels." In a second, more salacious photo, the fun-loving prince was photographed from behind as he playfully hugs a young woman—both are completely naked. While celebrity tabloids from around the world had fun exposing the young prince, the royal family was not amused. In fact, aides to Prince Charles threatened to sue any newspaper in England that published the photos.

This was not the first time that an English monarch felt threatened by the reporting of a free and independent press. Indeed, from the very birth of modern journalism, kings, emperors, and sovereigns have sought to control and limit public access to information that might challenge the dignity, authority, and power of the throne. The following ruling from an English court in 1680 is representative of this position: "His Majesty may by law prohibit the printing of all newsbooks and pamphlets of news whatsoever not licensed by his Majesty's authority as manifestly tending to the breach of the peace and disturbance of the kingdom."[2] One might assume that attempts to control public information disappeared with the emergence of democratic forms of government and the recognized value of a free press, but in fact objections to newspapers and other forms of communication, entertainment, and artistic expression appear regularly throughout history. Consider the following illustrative examples:[3]

- During the early nineteenth century, elite educators and clergymen were worried about the growing popularity of "the novel," which at the time was a new form of literary expression. Fiction was considered dangerous, not only because it "painted unreal pictures of human life," but also because it was thought to "enervate the youthful mind, and give it a disrelish for substantial and profitable reading."[4]
- As early as 1915 the motion picture industry was defending itself in the U.S. Congress against charges that movies were making young people emotionally unstable, retarding intelligence, promoting illiteracy, and contributing to delinquency and crime. The scandalous films from this era seem mild, even comical, by today's standards, but official censoring boards were formed throughout the United States to identify and limit offensive content.
- In 1954 the U.S. Senate subcommittee on juvenile delinquency initiated an investigation of the comic book industry. They were in fact responding to a public outcry against stories and images that involved crime, sexual innuendo, and violence. A national movement to censor comic books had formed, and organizations throughout the country were collecting and destroying the likes of *Superman* and *Batman* in public bonfires. Local jurisdictions passed anti-comic ordinances, and within a few years twenty-four crime comic publishers were forced out of business.
- Concern for the mental health of young people was the primary motivation in 1969 for the formation of the U.S. Surgeon General's

Scientific Advisory Committee on Television and Social Behavior. The committee was charged with investigating the impact of television violence. It resulted in two years of congressional hearings, a five-volume scientific report, and a set of highly qualified findings. The general conclusion was that viewing violence might increase aggressive behavior among some people under certain conditions.

- More recently, video games have been the target of public concern and government regulation. In March of 2012 the "Violence in Video Games Labeling Act" was introduced in the U.S. House of Representatives. The proposed law would require the display of the following notice on all packaging: "WARNING: Exposure to violent video games has been linked to aggressive behavior." According to one of the bills sponsors, "The video game industry has a responsibility to parents, families and to consumers—to inform them of the potentially damaging content that is often found in their products. They have repeatedly failed to live up to this responsibility."[5]

Newspapers, books, magazines, comics, television, radio, movies, records, video games, the Internet, MP3 players, and smart phones are all examples of what sociologists refer to as mass media—forms of communication that reach a large audience. In each of the cases summarized above, we see illustrations of mass media generating public concern, anxiety, and fear. From the invention of the printing press, to the discovery of radio waves, and up to the development of the World Wide Web, a segment of the public has worried about the unregulated power of new forms of communication and expression. Some of the negative reactions represent moral crusades by religious leaders and pious community members; some are energized by conservative politicians claiming to uphold the common good; and others reflect more rational interpretations of scientific research. But all share a common assumption that mass media are a powerful force in society with the potential to do harm.

In this chapter we will explore the power of mass media from a sociological perspective. How extensive are mass media in modern society? How do mass media shape our lives? Who controls mass media? After addressing these questions, we will briefly examine the mass media in relation to sex, violence, and politics, three topics that have generated public attention and concern since the very first newspaper was printed.

THE REACH OF MASS MEDIA

History tells us that Prince Harry was not the first English monarch to invite scandal while having a little naked fun with friends. King James I (1566–1625) was by all accounts bisexual and had several male lovers. Charles II (1630–1685) fathered at least fourteen illegitimate children with more than a dozen mistresses. Queen Caroline of Brunswick (1768–1821) engaged in several sexual affairs across Europe and, like Prince Harry, was reported to have stripped off all of her clothes at a royal party. One difference between Harry and his regal ancestors, however, is that for the first one thousand years of rule, the English Crown did not have to worry about cell phones and the Internet.

Although Prince Harry and the rest of the British royals live wealthy and privileged lives that continue to be subsidized by the citizens of the United Kingdom, Queen Elizabeth and her family are essentially figureheads with limited power and a status more akin to movie celebrities. In fact, the all-powerful sovereign of the eighteenth century began to crumble at about the same time that mass media started to emerge. As public communication grew from a few locally distributed pamphlets to an enormously complex and tangled network of expression, common people found a new resource for exposing corrupt power, communicating grievances, and agitating for democracy. In this sense, mass media helped promote positive social change by carving out a new space for discussion and debate among equals. Sociologists refer to this trend as the development of the public sphere.

Today the public sphere is still a space for political dialogue, but it is also the site of home entertainment videos, family photographs, online games, billions of dollars of advertising, celebrity rumors, pornography, shopping, virtual communities, dating services, music, and many other types of expression that have very little to do with political power. Communication among people in public places has always included music, entertainment, gossip, athletic competition, and political discourse but never with the scope and speed that we see today. Indeed, the reach of mass media has become so extensive, diverse, and constant that it is difficult to find any place or any person in the world that does not have some regular exposure to media on a daily basis. Media have literally become part of our everyday environment. This is especially true in the United States.

For example, a national survey conducted in 2009 found that the average high school–age student in the United States spends over eleven hours a day exposed to mass media—not including school-related assignments. Considering the fact that we are only awake for about sixteen hours a day, it is clear that mass media are a dominant feature of young people's lives. What is even more startling is the fact that in 2004, the average media exposure was only nine hours, which means that there was a two-hour increase in mass media exposure in just five years. In 2009 the typical fifteen- to eighteen-year-old spent four to five hours watching television, two to three hours listening to music, and about two hours surfing the web or playing video games. And these numbers do not account for time spent texting or talking on a cell phone. Moreover, much of this exposure involves acts of simultaneous multitasking where more than one type of medium is being used at a time, such as texting while listening to the radio, listening to music while playing a video game, or watching television while surfing the web.[6]

The following figures provide additional evidence of the dominance of mass media in modern society.

779,731: Average daily print circulation of the *New York Times* in 2012.

807,026: Average daily digital circulation for the *New York Times* in 2012.

302,000,000: The number of televisions in the United States in 2012.

56: The percent of households with three or more televisions in the United States.

71: The percent of eight- to eighteen-year-olds in the United States with a TV in their bedroom.

6,000,000: The number of U.S. middle and high school students who are required to watch the Channel One news program (including advertising) during class time.

19,000,000: The number of people who watched the NBC television broadcast of the 2012 Summer Olympics.

2,000,000,000: The number of website page views for the 2012 Summer Olympics.

190,000,000: The number of U.S. households with a video game console in 2012.

9,100,000: Number of subscribers to *World of Warcraft* (an online video game).

35: Average age of video game purchaser.

3,000,000,000: Number of hours per week spent playing video games across the globe.

20,000: Total number of magazines in U.S. circulation.

28,000,000: The number of songs available for download on iTunes in 2012.

15,000,000,000: Number of songs sold by iTunes as of June 2011.

4,000,000,000: Average number of YouTube views in one day.

2,612,826,709,119: Total YouTube views as of January 2012.

500,000,000: Number of views for YouTube video "Charlie Bit My Finger."

955,000,000: Number of active Facebook users as of June 2012.

109: The average number of text messages exchanged per day by eighteen- to twenty-four-year-olds in 2011.

14,528: The number of text messages exchanged in one month by a thirteen-year-old California girl in 2009.

DO THE MASS MEDIA HAVE THE POWER TO CONTROL US?

Given the ubiquity of exposure to mass media in our everyday lives, it is reasonable to assume that mass media have an effect on the attitudes and actions of people in modern society. Ask yourself, would Nike spend over two billion dollars a year on marketing if mass media advertising didn't cause people to buy Nike products? Would candidates for the U.S. presidency spend over four hundred million dollars on television ads (combined) if mass media didn't produce more votes and increase politicians' chances of getting elected? In fact, most of us are willing to admit that media images and messages do influence the attitudes and actions of other people. However, we are much less likely to think that our own behavior is being manipulated. Ask yourself, for example, whether or not you believe that sexual behaviors depicted on TV have an influence on the sexual behaviors of young people. Now ask yourself if you think that sexual behaviors on TV have an influence on your own sexual behavior. A study conducted in 2002 posed these same two questions to a sample of young people and found that 72 percent thought that TV did in fact affect sexual behavior of other young people, but only 22 percent claimed that it had any effect on their own actions.[7] In other words we can recognize the power of mass media when it controls other people, but we are unwilling to admit (or unable to recognize) the command that media might have over our own lives.

Several years ago I was holding a mandatory discussion session for an introductory sociology course. When one of my students failed to attend for the third meeting in a row, I asked the class if anyone knew what was going on with Russell (not his real name). This was the fall term; everyone in the group was a first-year student, and most were housed together in the same residence hall on campus. My question was answered with a few chuckles, several mutual glances, and some eye rolling, but no one admitted to knowing anything about Russell's whereabouts. Once class was over, however, and the room was mostly empty, Russell's roommate, who was also in the class, approached me with an anxious look on his face. In a halting voice, and with a quick glance over his shoulder, he offered to fill me in on Russell's situation: "Russell is in trouble, he whispered, I think . . . uh . . . that he might have a serious addiction." Over my many years of teaching I have had quite a few students with out-of-control drug problems, so I wasn't entirely surprised. But what Russell's friend told me next was hard for me to believe. "It's not drugs," he said. "It's just that he won't stop playing *World of Warcraft*. He doesn't go to class anymore, he rarely eats, and he plays all through the night." For a second I thought he was joking with me, but the look on his face was grave, and I could tell he was concerned. I was not familiar with this video game, but I learned that it was an online, massive, multiplayer role-playing journey in which players guide a personal avatar on adventure quests while negotiating alliances with other participants. I was skeptical and wondered to myself whether it was even possible for someone to become addicted to a video game. Later in the week Russell himself approached me and confessed that he did indeed feel like he needed help. In fact, he ended up getting counseling and later dropped out of school. Whether *World of Warcraft* caused this student's academic failure is hard to know, but Russell certainly thought so.

A few years later I ran across a book written by an English professor in which he describes his own personal struggle to kick a *World of Warcraft* habit that had reached sixty hours a week of playing time. The manuscript details the author's downward spiral from successful college professor, husband, and father to an unemployed, suicidal man, on the verge of losing his family. In explaining the lure of the game, the thirty-eight-year-old describes how "playing WoW makes me feel god-like, I have ultimate control and can do what I want with few real repercussions. The real world makes me feel impotent . . . a computer malfunction, a sobbing child, a suddenly dead cell phone battery—the littlest hitch in daily living feels profoundly disempowering."[8] But, of course, the irony evident in this quote is that while the video game might have generated feelings of empowerment, in the real world the game was actually altering this young man's mood, disrupting his social relationships, and reconfiguring his daily habits.

Sociologists do not typically employ the word addiction. This is because addiction is a concept that focuses almost exclusively on the individual and tends to rely on physiological explanations of behavior. The idea of addiction might be useful in making sense of extreme behavior for some people, but it cannot capture the larger social patterns and social forces that represent the environment within which addictions emerge. Sociologists believe that we cannot fully understand human behavior unless social context is taken into account. Think, for example, about cigarettes. This particular drug is, without a doubt, habit forming. Smoking cigarettes produces a physiological change that can alter body chemistry and lead to cravings. If longtime smokers attempt to quit, they experience symptoms of withdrawal, become irritable, feel sick, and get depressed. In other words, nicotine is addictive. But this is only part of the story. In the background is another tale of a powerful global industry that produces over six trillion cigarettes a year. Before any one person can become addicted to cigarettes, farm owners must be paid to grow tobacco; workers must be paid to harvest tobacco; factories must be constructed to manufacture cigarettes; corporations must design attractive packaging; retailers must agree to stock and sell the product; distributers must ship the product around the globe; marketing campaigns must be designed to attract customers; political influence must be deployed to protect the industry from its critics; and mass media must be used to advertise the product. In 2008, about $10 billion was spent by tobacco companies on advertising cigarettes, and in 2010, tobacco companies spent about $17 million and employed close to two hundred lobbyists in an attempt to influence legislation in the United States.[9]

We can talk about being addicted to video games, having television withdrawal, or experiencing cravings for Facebook, but for sociologists, the effects of mass media are much more complicated than this. The power of mass media emerges from many different locations while discretely enveloping us like an early morning fog. Its effects are often subtle, stealthy, and tangled up with other forms of control. For this reason, the power of mass media is difficult to isolate, hard to measure, and a challenge to study. Most young people who read comic books will not become juvenile delinquents; very few children who watch television will develop sexual perversions; and the vast majority of video gamers do not flunk out of school. But this does not mean that mass media are not having an influence. In the following section we will take a closer look at the effects of mass media in three areas: violence, sex, and politics.

VIOLENCE

When I was around nine or ten years old, my brothers and I would rise early on Saturday morning, gulp down our breakfast cereal, and head straight for the family television set. Crowded together on the floor in our pajamas, we would wait anxiously in anticipation of our favorite show. In the early 1960s, television programming was not nearly as extensive as it is today. There were only three stations with a handful of cartoons, and all programs were in black and white. But Saturday was special; on this day the network would broadcast replays of a 1940s movie series about a noble hero in the jungles of Africa who wore only a loincloth and was unchained from the conventions of civilization—it was time for Tarzan! Each film-episode promised great adventure with titles such as "Tarzan Escapes!" "Tarzan's Secret Treasure!" and even "Tarzan and His Mate!" We would watch in amazement as Tarzan swung on jungle vines from tree to tree, wrestled tigers and pythons to their death, and communicated with all animal species using his distinctive jungle yell. Each week, for a little over an hour, we would sit silently, like zombies, eyes transfixed, oblivious to our surroundings. But soon after the final credits started to roll, we would emerge from our media-induced daze, and all hell would break lose. Without hesitation, we would rip off our pajama tops, pound our chest like great apes, mimic Tarzan's yell, and start to leap from chair to chair. Weather permitting, we would take our role-playing game outside where we would climb trees in our bare feet and fashion sticks into knives. More than once our fun would get out of hand: wrestling would turn into fighting, older brothers would pick on younger brothers, and someone would end up in tears. When this occurred, our parents would inevitably threaten us with an unspeakably cruel punishment—no more Tarzan!

I share this story for several reasons. First it provides an example of how media images and fictional stories might encourage aggressive play among young people—something all of us have experienced or noticed at some level. Second, it serves as a caution against hyperbole and overreaction; Tarzan did not turn us into delinquents, and none of us ever ended up committing a serious crime of violence. Third, it hints at the complexity of the relationship between media content and audience response. If watching one mildly violent show can promote aggressive play, what is the effect of many television shows, movies, and video games combined over the course of a lifetime?

My childhood experience with Tarzan is an example of what social psychologists refer to as a priming effect. The basic idea is that media images prime thoughts and ideas that set the stage for behavior modeled after the same images. In other words, the aggressive and athletic actions of Tarzan triggered aggressive ideas in my head, which then led to my aggressive play. The fact that my brothers had also been primed in exactly the same way served to fuel the fire of aggression. This is a rather simple explanation for how movies, video games, and TV might promote violence. In fact, there is a solid body of research in support of this idea. For example, back in 1995, when *Power Rangers* was the most popular children's television show, researchers conducted an experiment with a group of five- to eleven-year-olds who were participating in an after-school program. On the first day of the study, researchers closely watched the group at play and counted the incidences of verbal and physical aggression displayed by each child. The next day the researchers randomly divided the group in half: twenty-six children were allowed to watch an episode of *Power Rangers*, but the other twenty-six were not. At the time of the study, *Power Rangers* was rated the most violent children's show on television, and so the researchers were expecting it to produce a priming effect. After the episode was over (about twenty minutes) the two groups were reunited for playtime. Once again the number of acts of aggression were counted. Did the children who were exposed to *Power Rangers* play more aggressively than the control group? Yes, in fact, the difference between the groups was quite large. The kids who watched *Power Rangers* committed seven aggressive acts for every one aggressive act committed by the students in the control group. This effect, however, was much more pronounced for boys than it was for girls.[10]

In another study, interviews were conducted with a random sample of young people between the ages of sixteen and twenty. The researchers asked a series of questions about health, risky behavior, lifestyle, family background, and media consumption, with a special focus on how often the young people watched televised wrestling. The findings showed that regular viewers of wrestling (six times per week) were 144 percent more likely to get into a date fight, 119 percent more likely to have threatened someone with a weapon, and 184 percent more likely to have tried to hurt someone with a weapon. And while males watched wrestling more often than females, the women who watched wrestling were just as likely as the men to report engaging in violent behavior. These results were found even after controlling for differences in background variables such as family income, region of the country, and race.[11]

There are other examples of research where violent television shows, video games, and movies are shown to promote aggressive behavior.[12] But we need to be careful not to overgeneralize from a single study or two. The actual consequence of a particular medium or program on a specific person is very difficult to predict. Nevertheless, when we consider the full range of mass media that we are exposed to on a daily basis, and take into account the extraordinary number of violent acts that they portray (it is estimated that the average child witnesses over two hundred thousand acts of violence and sixteen thousand murders before the age of eighteen), we can be confident in concluding that the media environment of modern society does in fact increase the overall likelihood of aggressive behavior in a society. While this conclusion may not come as a surprise to many, there is another effect of media violence that is less well recognized and may in fact be even more powerful. I am referring here to evidence that mass media produces a widespread sense of trepidation, concern, and fear of violence among regular consumers.

In Alfred Hitchcock's film *Psycho*, there is an iconic scene in which a woman is stabbed to death in a shower. The depiction is rather tame by today's movie standards, but when I first saw it at about eleven or twelve years of age, I was terrified. Days passed before I was able to take a shower in the evening without experiencing anxiety and nervousness. Some years later, I had a similar experience after watching *The Exorcist* during my first year in college. My roommate and I left the theater joking about devil possession and projectile vomiting, but neither of us slept a wink that night, and to this day I avoid watching replays of the film—especially if it is showing late at night. I'll admit I may be a bit more skittish than the average man, but the sociological evidence suggests that I am not alone.

One of the more consistent findings in mass media research is that high levels of media exposure are associated with beliefs that the world is a mean, scary, and violent place. This seems to be especially true for people who watch a good deal of television. Several studies, for example, find that watching crime dramas on TV is related to an increased fear of becoming a crime victim. And a recent study found that among American college students, watching more local television news was associated with higher levels of fear.[13] This may explain why Americans believe that crime is a growing problem despite clear evidence that crime rates have been declining for some time. For example, when a national sample of Americans was asked recently "Is there more or less crime in the U.S. than there was a year ago?" 66 percent said that there is more crime, and only 17 percent thought that there was less crime. Most people were wrong. The truth is that the national violent crime rate is about half of what it was in 1990, while property crime is about 40 percent lower over the same period. According to the National Archive of Criminal Justice Data, these numbers have been going down at a fairly steady pace for the past twenty years. However, every year since 1989, most Americans have told pollsters that they believe crime is getting worse.[14]

In many ways, the media environment is more influential than our actual physical environment. We appear to rely more on TV than on our own personal experience when establishing our beliefs. It is as if we are saying to ourselves, "If examples of crime continue to be sensationalized on the news, and crime dramas continue to display violence at an escalating pace, well, then crime must be going up. Right?" While it might be possible to dismiss these findings as harmless examples of people living in a make-believe world, the consequences of these irrational beliefs can be significant. We know, for example, that adults who have an elevated fear of crime are more likely to support increased funding for police and prisons, and are more likely to favor forms of severe punishment such as the death penalty. When the media have the power to establish false representations of reality, exploitation and manipulation of the public is not far behind.

SEX

As I noted above, the Saturday morning Tarzan series was a popular program in my family when I was growing up. But this is only half the truth. It is important to acknowledge that my sisters did not exhibit the same level of enthusiasm for the show. In retrospect this is not surprising. Tarzan was written and produced by men, it featured a strong male protagonist in the lead role, and many story lines involved Tarzan's adopted son—aptly named Boy—who was basically a younger version of Tarzan. Women and girls were not central to most plots. Tarzan's "mate" was an Englishwoman named Jane. Tarzan loved Jane, he protected her from harm, and rescued her when necessary, but her character was mostly subservient, weak, and in most scenes, dependent on men. In other words, the Tarzan movies were like most media of the era—they presented sexist stereotypes of women.

My sisters all turned out to be strong, independent women with professional careers. They are no more like Jane than my brothers and I are like Tarzan. So one might ask, What's the big deal? Can't women choose to ignore sexist media? Won't movie and TV producers create positive representations of women when they realize that stereotyped images are bad for business? After all, wasn't *The Hunger Games* the top grossing film of 2012? These are all legitimate points. There is no doubt that there are many positive images of women in contemporary media. We can see this, for example, in fictional characters from Katniss Everdeen (*The Hunger Games*) to major media moguls like Oprah Winfrey. Still, we must be cautious. The media environment is complex and multifaceted, and the power of mass media is often subtle and hard to detect. But if we look carefully, and with an analytical perspective, these hidden effects can be detected. This can be illustrated with the following example.

In the summer of 2011 *Rolling Stone* magazine featured a lengthy essay by Al Gore—former vice president and winner of both a Nobel Peace Prize and an Academy Award. The title of the piece was "Climate of Denial: Can Science and the Truth Withstand the Merchants of Poison?" It is a provocative and compelling critique of the news media, political ideologues, the corporate energy industry, and the collective failure of all three groups to advance the truth on issues of global warming. The article is well written, informative, and convincing. I have no doubt that it had a positive influence on readers' attitudes about the politics of climate change. However, I am also absolutely certain that the magazine's cover photo of Katy Perry generated more public attention and discussion than Al Gore's essay. The pop singer and music video diva is photographed from the waist up with her body in profile and her face, slightly tilted backward, turned toward the camera. Her long, black hair falls naturally down her back, and her dark, red lips frame a mouth that is halfway opened. It is an intentionally sexy pose that is accented by a wardrobe designed to emphasize this interpretation. The young star is wearing a glistening, silver halter-top bikini with a plunging neckline. But this is no ordinary bikini. The material covering each breast is twisted to simulate the foil candy wrapping of a chocolate Kiss. And just in case the message might not be clear, two white ribbons are dangling from the end of each breast with the same lettering found on the candies, only in this case they read, Katy's Kisses.

If you are a reader of *Rolling Stone* magazine, you know that the cover photos are usually provocative and often feature highly sexualized images of young celebrities. If you are as old as I am, and started reading the magazine thirty or forty years ago, it may seem as though the covers have become more sensational and salacious over the years. Sociologists Erin Hatton and Mary Nell Trautner, in fact, examined this question in a study published in 2011.[15] Following up on other research that suggested a growing sexualization or "pornification" of mass media, they wanted to see if *Rolling Stone* cover images were becoming increasingly sexualized and whether or not there were any differences in the representation of men and women. To do this, they first developed a measurement strategy for rating the degree to which an image could be considered sexualized. This involved a point system for eleven different variables, including amount of nudity, style of clothing, type of touching, if it was a head or full body shot, and so forth. The researchers then rated all magazine covers from 1967 to 2009 (a total of 1,006). The results are summarized below:

- In the 1960s, 11 percent of men and 44 percent of women on the covers of *Rolling Stone* were sexualized at some level.
- In the 2000s, 17 percent of men were sexualized (a 55 percent increase), and 83 percent of women were sexualized (an 89 percent increase) at some level.
- 2 percent of men were "hypersexualized" (sexualization score in the top half).
- 61 percent of women were "hypersexualized."

This means that there has been an increase in the sexualization of both men and women but that the sexualization of women is greater, has increased faster, and is more extreme. The conclusion, according to the authors, is that while men are more likely to be portrayed as "sexy," women are increasingly portrayed as "ready and available for sex."

Other researchers have drawn similar conclusions after analyzing the role of gender in mass media advertising. One perceptive analyst who has been particularly effective in showing how advertising affects our understanding of gender is Jean Kilbourne. For the past thirty years she has "deconstructed" hundreds of ads to expose a consistent pattern of manipulation and exploitation on the part of big businesses. Some key points from her research are as follows:

- Women who appear as models in advertising are unrepresentative of most women (only 5 percent have similar body types). Their bodies and faces are often artificially manipulated and digitally enhanced in an effort to present an unreachable ideal. If the consumer falls short in comparison, the advertised product can be presented as a solution to the problem.
- Images of women often focus on parts of the body or equate women with animals (e.g., in a cage or crawling on all fours). This can have the effect of objectifying and dehumanizing women, which can facilitate and legitimate violent attitudes and actions.
- Women are often positioned in submissive or passive poses in relation to men. This can create the expectation that women should be silent and docile, especially in relationship to men.
- The cumulative consequence for our understanding of gender in our culture is negative. Ads reinforce harmful ideals of what it means to be masculine and manly, and what it means to be feminine and womanly. For both men and women, it can mean the trivialization of sex and relationships, a warping of body image and self-esteem, and an increase in emotional and physical violence.

In books, videos, and public presentations Dr. Kilbourne uses her research to deliver two messages. First, advertising is a powerful and harmful force in society that often changes how we think and feel. Second, we are not helpless dopes in the face of advertising. If we pay attention, and are aware of the intended manipulation, we can use a critical attitude to resist and limit its negative effects.

Still, you might be asking yourself, How does advertising work to change people's beliefs and behaviors? This is a complicated question, and we don't have all of the answers at this point, but one thing we do know is that advertising relies on the power of pictures. You may be familiar with the expression "A picture is worth a thousand words." This phrase is intended to suggest that a photograph is more efficient in transmitting information than either the written or spoken word. In other words, we can look at a photograph and instantly "understand" what we see. But this adage misses a more significant difference between words and images. A photograph represents a world of objects, while language represents a world of ideas. Neil Postman (1931–2003), an insightful critic of modern media, explains:

> Language makes sense only when it is presented as a sequence of propositions. Meaning is distorted when a word or sentence is, as we say, taken out of context; when a reader or listener is deprived of what was said before, or after. But there is no such thing as a photograph taken out of context, for a photograph does not require one. In fact, the point of photography is to isolate images from context, so as to make them visible in a different way. [16]

Photographs and words have different functions, they transfer different types of meanings, and they are used to do different things. The written word can be used to make logical arguments, to present evidence, and to engage the reader in a rational analysis. But this takes time, patience, and usually a space free from distractions. The photograph, on the other hand, is brief, instant, and is used to provoke an immediate response that depends on emotion and arousal. It usually requires only a brief glance, a few seconds of time, and no real effort. This helps explain why Katy Perry's cover photo on *Rolling Stone* may have had a greater public impact than Al Gore's article. It also explains why ads are dominated by photographs and provocative images, and use only a few words when promoting a product. And finally, it can help us understand how forces that are mostly concealed from view have the power to influence our assumptions and expectations about gender relations. When mass media are so dominant in our lives, and when advertising images are so dominant within mass media, advertising images become part of our cultural environment.

In the end, the primary goal of advertisers is not to change our culture or to provide entertainment; these are secondary consequences. The first and most important goal is to sell products and make a profit.

Advertisers spend more than $250 billion in a single year to intentionally manipulate consumers' preferences. This means that much of the power of mass media is in the hands of a small percentage of the population that produces and controls big business. But this level of domination by a small elite is not inevitable, and as we will see in the next section, mass media can also be used as a tool for resistance and positive political change.

POLITICS

December 10, 2010, began as a typical day for Mohamed Bouazizi, a twenty-six-year-old street vendor from a small city in the North Africa country of Tunisia. He rose early, loaded a small cart with fruits and vegetables, and traveled the short distance from his modest home to the city center where he set up shop at around 8:00 a.m. According to eyewitnesses, within a few hours local police approached Mohamed, confiscated the scales he used to weigh his produce, turned over his cart, and issued him a small fine. This was not the first time Mohamed had been confronted by authorities, and family members insist that the actions of the police were consistent with a regular pattern of extortion. On this day, however, Mohamed did not back down. He had no money to pay the fine, so he appealed to local officials and demanded that his scales be returned. Security officials responded by beating him. He then went to the office of the regional governor. Once again he was rebuffed, and once again security personnel assaulted him. Humiliated in public and frustrated by government officials, Mohamed grabbed a can of gasoline, stood in front of the governor's office, and shouted, "How do you expect me to make a living!" He then poured the fuel over his head, lit a match, and set himself on fire. He suffered severe burns over 90 percent of his body and died a few weeks later in the hospital.

If not for the events that followed, Mohamed's suicide would have gone unnoticed outside of his local community. Instead, he is recognized today as the catalyst of a political revolution in his home country of Tunisia and is renowned as the inspiration for a series of uprisings and revolutions that occurred across the Middle East throughout 2011 and into 2012. This momentous historical period has come to be known as the Arab Spring, and it encompasses an amazing succession of democratically inspired revolts that saw the toppling of dictators and military regimes that had controlled the region for decades. Table 6.1 summarizes the magnitude of this historical moment.

In addition, during this same time period, major uprisings occurred in Morocco, Saudi Arabia, Bahrain, Jordan, Lebanon, and Syria. Some of these protests produced major political reforms while others were still political hot spots at the time of this writing in 2012.

Table 6.1.

Date	Country	Ruler removed	Years in power
01/14/2011	Tunisia	Zine al-Abidine Ben Ali	23
02/11/2011	Egypt	Hosni Mubarak	29
08/28/2011	Libya	Muammar al-Qaddafi	32
02/27/2012	Yemen	Ali Abdullah Saleh	22

So how did one man's desperate act of self-immolation trigger rebellion, reform, and revolution throughout the Arab world? How was it possible for a poor street vendor to inspire uprisings in city streets more than three thousand miles from his own hometown? The answer is complex and involves many factors. But we do know that this region has some of the least democratic governments in the world and was already at a tipping point for social change. Mohamed was not a social activist or political insurgent. He did not intend to become a martyr or an inspirational symbol. But when other similarly frustrated and angry citizens learned of Mohamed's tragic death, saw images of his burned body, and shared stories of comparable deprivations and humiliations, a cascade of information began to flood the public sphere. In other words, mass media was instrumental in spreading the word, identifying grievances, and organizing revolt.

Historians and social scientists have long known that dictators, monarchs, and political tyrants must control the mass media if they are to maintain their grip on power. This is why television, newspapers, and radio stations are closely supervised and carefully censored by authoritarian governments. And this is also why rebels attempt to wrestle control of the mass media from the hands of government autocrats. But what happens if mass media are not centrally located and controlled? How can an undemocratic regime stifle popular protest if people have access to the Internet and cell phones? In fact, one of the lessons from the Arab Spring is that modern communication technologies are increasingly difficult to manage. Indeed, many social scientists believe that the period of revolution we are presently experiencing in the Middle East and North Africa is due in large part to the effectiveness of the Internet and cell phones as tools for organizing against dictatorships and for advancing a more open and democratic public sphere.

Let's return to the case of Mohamed Bouazizi and take a closer look and how these tools were used to construct a chain of revolutions. Almost immediately after Mohamed set himself on fire, friends and sympathetic bystanders that had witnessed the event took to the street. "An ambulance took him away, and people starting gathering," said one witness. "By the afternoon it was a demonstration, and the police intervened with clubs and tear gas."[17] Shortly thereafter, cell phone photos taken at the hospital began to appear on Facebook. The pictures showed Mohamed's charred body wrapped from head to toe in bandages. The images and story of an extraordinary act taken by an ordinary street vendor spread quickly among friends and family, and soon an online campaign was calling on citizens to support the protest. Students were among the first and largest group to join the demonstrations, and their videos and images of the police backlash were also circulated among an even larger social network. The government realized it had a problem and called for a ban on Facebook, Twitter, YouTube, and other online sites where the protest was being shared and organized. But in Tunisia only 20 percent of the population are regular users of social media, so cutting off the Internet was not sufficient. The most powerful organizing tool turned out to be text messages circulated via cell phones. Within a few weeks the government appeared to have lost control of the streets. Protests spread rapidly to the Tunisian capital, and violent clashes between citizens and the military were occurring in other major cities. Then, on January 4, eighteen days after he set himself on fire, Mohamed Bouazizi was pronounced dead. His funeral procession became an epic march in a revolutionary movement and the site of another public demonstration. His body was gone, but his story survived as a symbol of resistance. Ten days later, the country's dictator, Zine al-Abidine Ben Ali, fearing for his life, fled to Saudi Arabia. His ouster led to democratic elections and a new government in Tunisia.

News of the success of the Tunisian uprising spread quickly to other countries in the region where authoritarian governments were also ensconced in power. Once again, information, images, and discussions bypassed television, radio, and newspapers because these traditional forms of mass media were tightly controlled and censored by the state.

In Egypt, for example, where the Internet is widely available and most citizens own a cell phone, protests began to grow at a rapid pace. While Mohamed Bouazizi was an inspiration in this country, Egyptians also had their own heroes and martyrs whose stories and images were more locally relevant. As was the case in Tunisia, Facebook, Twitter, and text messaging were used to link networks of people who shared grievances, hopes for a better world, and strategies for radical democratic reform. On January 25, 2011, a mass demonstration was organized for the main public square in the capital city of Cairo. This event was risky—if protesters were outnumbered by the military, the unarmed citizens would likely be arrested and imprisoned; but if thousands showed up and flooded the square with demonstrators, there would be security in numbers and authorities would have a difficult time making arrests. To the surprise of observers from around the world, and to the shock of Egypt's authoritarian government, over fifty thousand demonstrators arrived at the square. In fact, the protest continued to grow with each passing day. After a week, independent media were reporting crowds in excess of three hundred thousand. Hosni Mubarak, the longtime autocrat of Egypt, recognized that the Internet was a threat and tried to have the network shut down. But his efforts backfired. Businesses and government agencies became paralyzed, anger grew over the leader's desperate act, and tech-savvy rebels found alternate routes around the chokehold. Security officials also sought to identify, intimidate, detain, and torture bloggers and Facebook posters who were critical of the government, but these efforts also proved unsuccessful. Help arrived from other regions of the world in the form of electronic advice and tips on how to organize mass demonstrations using text messaging and Twitter. Mubarak soon realized that he had lost control of the country, and on February 11, 2012, after twenty-nine years of autocratic rule, he resigned as president. He was then promptly arrested by the new provisional government and was charged with the murder of peaceful protesters.

Here it is important to emphasize that while Mohamed Bouazizi's desperate suicide sparked a wave of public protests, his lone act did not produce the revolutions that followed. Radical social change requires the cooperation of tens of thousands of people who must find a way to organize around common frustrations and grievances. As we saw in this chapter, the mass media can be a powerful tool for sharing provocative images and inciting violence, but in times of political repression they can also be a force for coordinating actions and communicating strategy. In the next chapter, we will explore the power of collective action in more detail when we examine the relationship between individuals and social movements that generate positive democratic change.

Chapter Seven

From "Me" to "We"

The Power of Collective Action

If there is no struggle there is no progress. Those who profess to favor freedom and yet deprecate agitation are men who want crops without plowing up the ground; they want rain without thunder and lightning. They want the ocean without the awful roar of its many waters. . . . Power concedes nothing without a demand. It never did and it never will.

—Frederick Douglass[1]

In the winter of 1861, Jefferson Davis, a fifty-three-year-old war veteran and former U.S. senator, stood on the steps of the state capitol building in Montgomery, Alabama, and gave his first speech as the president of the Confederate States of America. In his defiant stance against the U.S. government he proclaimed allegiance to a new union of southern militants committed to fighting a civil war in defense of "states' rights." At stake was the institution of slavery, a system of exploitation that sustained the plantation economy of the white population and structured the social relations of power throughout the southern half of the U.S. territory. The first shots of the American Civil War were still months away, but Montgomery, Alabama, was already the symbolic center of a proslavery insurgency.

Nearly four years and 630,000 deaths later, Jefferson Davis was captured at his hideout in Georgia, marking the end of the American Civil War. Although the military battles over the legality of slavery had

153

ceased, most white citizens of the South remained defiant. With the help of the Ku Klux Klan and other racist fraternal organizations, the white power structure continued to control, exploit, and denigrate black citizens for another century. Verbal intimidation, physical beatings, and murderous lynchings were regularly employed as weapons of terror in support of white power and a strictly enforced system of racial segregation. A century after the Thirteenth Amendment to the U.S. Constitution ended slavery, African Americans in the South were still legally excluded from white schools, barred from the political system, and relegated to subservient tasks in the economy. Although blacks regularly fought back, individual acts in defiance of the segregationist norms were met with swift and firm rebukes. Taking a personal stand in support of racial equality could mean losing one's job, a lengthy jail sentence, a physical assault, or even a tortuous death.

This was the harsh social context that structured Rosa Parks's life in 1955. As an African American she was well aware of the dangers she faced in her decision to defy the racist power structure of Montgomery, Alabama. It was a simple act of peaceful resistance, but it catapulted the quiet and courageous woman to the forefront of a perilous movement for civil rights. It would also reestablish Montgomery, Alabama, as the symbolic center of a national struggle over "states' rights"—only this time it was the black population taking a rebellious stand.

A WOMAN AND A MOVEMENT

When Rosa Parks awoke at the crack of dawn on December 1, 1955, she could not anticipate the momentous series of events that lay ahead. [2] It was in most ways a typical day for the forty-two-year-old seamstress. After spending the morning and afternoon sewing and ironing in the basement of the Montgomery Fair department store, she clocked out and started her short walk to the downtown bus stop to catch her usual ride home. Rosa Parks was not looking for a fight; her feet were tired, and her shoulders ached from a full day of grinding work. As she made her way to Court Square she was hemmed in by city shops that displayed a festive mood. The local stores were already adorned with Christmas lights and bright holiday decorations. Four blocks away, however, at the eastern end of Dexter Avenue, the Confederate battle flag fluttered atop the state capitol building, a stark reminder of white power and the enduring legacy of slavery.

When the Court Street bus pulled up to the curb, Rosa stepped on board, instinctively dropped her coin in the fare box, and headed for a bench behind the sign that read "colored." She settled into an aisle seat across from two other black women. Next to Rosa, in the window seat, sat a black man. By the time the passengers had boarded at the next stop, the front section of the bus was filled up, leaving a single white male standing. When Mrs. Parks and the other three passengers in the front of the colored section did not initially move out of their seats, the visibly perturbed bus driver turned and ordered them to stand. "Y'all better make it light on yourselves and let me have those seats." The two women sitting across the aisle from Rosa grudgingly acquiesced, as did the man sitting next to her. Rosa, however, remained seated. The bus fell quiet. Anticipating trouble, some passengers made their way to the exit doors. As the angry driver stood to demand obedience, Rosa slid over to the window seat and fixed her gaze on the marquee of the movie theater across the street. Terrifying memories of Ku Klux Klan violence flashed in front of her. "I thought back to the time when I used to sit up all night and didn't sleep, and my grandfather would have his gun right by the fireplace." Rosa decided to take a stand by staying seated. "Are you going to stand up!" the red-faced driver demanded. Rosa's response was a simple but firm "No."

Two Montgomery police officers arrived within minutes. As expected, Mrs. Parks was taken into custody, charged with violating the city's segregation laws, and placed behind bars in the city jail. A century earlier, African slaves were held in chains, physically inspected, and auctioned off with livestock from the very same downtown location where Parks boarded her bus. Rosa Parks was continuing the fight for freedom and justice that her ancestors had initiated more than two hundred years earlier.

Later that evening Rosa Parks was released on bond. When she arrived with her husband and friends for her trial on Monday morning, a crowd of five hundred supporters had assembled at that courthouse. Even though no one expected Rosa Parks to prevail in court, the throng of African American observers reacted with a collective moan of frustration and anger when the guilty verdict was handed down. A planned boycott of the city bus system was already in the works, and a mass community meeting was scheduled for later in the evening at the Holt Street Baptist Church. At that meeting a charismatic, twenty-six-year-old preacher by the name of Martin Luther King Jr. would be selected to lead a new civic organization demanding changes in the Montgomery transit service: (1) more courteous treatment of blacks; (2) blacks would not have to give up seats in the colored section; and (3) black bus drivers would be hired to drive the routes in black neighborhoods.

What began as a minor local arrest of a respected African American woman would eventually give rise to the most historic period of advocacy for civil rights in the history of America. The bus boycott would last for more than a year as media from across the globe turned their attention to Montgomery, Alabama. Similar boycotts and sit-ins in defiance of segregation sprung up throughout the South. The Reverend King and other boycott activists would eventually lead a national civil rights movement that would fight on the streets and in the courts for racial integration, voting rights, and an end to poverty.

When Rosa Parks passed away in 2005 at the age of ninety-two, her funeral was attended by dignitaries from around the world. She was hailed as a great heroine whose "actions and conduct changed the face of the nation."[3] Her casket was taken to Washington, D.C., and placed in the capitol rotunda building where fifty thousand mourners processed through to pay their respects. Before her death she was awarded the Presidential Medal of Freedom and the Congressional Gold Medal. Her home state of Alabama recognized her historic achievements with the Governor's Medal of Honor for Extraordinary Courage. The yellow transit bus on which Rosa Parks took her stand against racial injustice is now preserved at the Henry Ford Museum in Detroit, Michigan. Cleveland Avenue in Montgomery has been renamed Rosa Parks Boulevard, and the corner of downtown Montgomery where Parks boarded the bus in 1955 is now home to the Rosa Parks Library and Museum.

There is no doubt that Rosa Parks is one of the most iconic individuals in American history. She is known as the "mother of the civil rights movement"—for good reason. Young people today who read about Rosa Parks in their history books are often inspired and motivated to take a stand in support of justice and equality—and it would be difficult to find a more worthy role model. Nevertheless, there is a problem with the way the Rosa Parks story is usually told. The narrative typically follows the same series of events and personal descriptions that I have outlined above—Rosa's strength of character, her confrontation with the bus driver, and the inspiration she brought to her community. But the trouble with this familiar account is that it is incomplete; it is a narrow telling that emphasizes a single act by a lone individual. Like many well-known historical depictions, the Rosa Parks story, as told by popular media and classroom textbooks, deemphasizes the role of collective action and ignores the years of planning, organizing, and training that preceded her act. Rosa Parks would be the first to acknowledge that no single individual is responsible for sparking the civil rights movement.

Racism in the United States is a by-product and servant of economic exploitation. Over time it has been sustained by the heavy hand of tradition, institutionalized through law, and enforced with physical violence, verbal abuse, and organized campaigns of intimidation. A single individual, no matter how strong, charismatic, intelligent, or persistent, could not be responsible for its defeat. The Montgomery bus boycott is often depicted as an emotional reaction ignited by Rosa Parks's arrest. But this explanation ignores the political context, organizational strategy, and collective action that prepared and propelled the boycott. As we saw in chapter 1, the culture of American individualism celebrates the power of individual people and deemphasizes the power of social forces. And when the Rosa Parks story is removed from its larger social context, we are seduced into believing that positive social change is dependent upon heroic figures. This is not true. Real change demands group solidarity, a shared consciousness, and a common, coordinated effort on the part of oppressed people acting together.

We can see this if we step back and take a broader look at Rosa Parks's life. When we examine the social environment that surrounded her personal act of resistance, our perspective becomes more inclusive and less biased. We learn, for example, that Rosa Parks and her husband, Raymond, were longtime activists with the National Association for the Advancement of Colored People (NAACP). The NAACP was at the time the most powerful organization in the country fighting for black civil rights, and Rosa Parks began serving as secretary for the Montgomery chapter in 1943. We learn that Rosa Parks was not the first black woman to be arrested for refusing to give up her seat to a white passenger. In Montgomery alone, there were three similar arrests earlier that same year, including Claudette Colvin, a high school student who was involved in the NAACP Youth Council led by Rosa Parks. We learn that Rosa Parks received leadership training at the Highlander Folk School in Tennessee. Funded by a scholarship from the NAACP, she spent two weeks during the summer of 1955 learning about "Radical Desegregation" with other left-wing political activists from around the country. We learn that Rosa Parks was a member of the Montgomery Voters League that worked to assist blacks in gaining access to the ballot box. We learn that Rosa Parks was a devout member of the St. Paul African Methodist Episcopal (AME) Church in Montgomery and that the AME was organized to protest against slavery and worked vigorously in support of African American civil rights. We also learn that Rosa Parks was involved in strategy discussions with other black community leaders about a possible boycott of the Montgomery bus system. All of this "radical organizing" occurred before she was arrested in 1955.

The important point here is that if we are to fully understand the story of Rosa Parks, we need to recognize that she was part of a much larger network of organized community activists with a long history in the African American community. This system of interlinked organizations and leaders included civil rights lawyers, labor unions, church ministers, students, educators, politicians, and poor people committed to changing their community. In sum, Rosa Parks was part of what sociologists call a "social movement."

WHAT IS A SOCIAL MOVEMENT?

A social movement is a particular type of collective action wherein ordinary people come together to challenge a dominant power structure. Unlike the actions of established political parties, social movement activity can be described as "contentious politics" because it includes public demonstrations, boycotts, marches, sit-ins, rallies, mass meetings, strikes, and other tactics that fall outside of established legislative proceedings or campaigns to elect a candidate. This does not mean that all forms of dissent against authority are to be considered a social movement. Short-lived protests that periodically flare up and disappear would be excluded from this definition because social movements require people with a common purpose to sustain their efforts over a significant period of time. In this way, a social movement should be thought of as a durable challenge to a dominant system of authority, with an identifiable history and a deeply committed group of supporters.

The story of Rosa Parks is significant because her actions are generally associated with the place and time when the American "civil rights movement" is believed to have begun. In truth, however, it is impossible to identify the precise historical boundaries of a social movement, just as it is impossible to identify the exact individuals and actions that define the movement. When a river overflows its banks and floods a town, it makes little sense to search for the particular rain drop responsible for the deluge. In much the same way, sociologists are not concerned with identifying the one individual responsible for the civil rights movement. If Rosa Parks had refused to relinquish her seat just a few months earlier, her courageous act might not have led to the Montgomery bus boycott. In the same way that a flood is preceded by days of stormy weather, a social movement gradually builds up pressure over time. It takes a history of exploitation and a collection of shared grievances before an identifiable social movement emerges.

In the case of the civil rights movement, some historians and most of the news media focus their attention on charismatic leaders, riveting events, violent confrontations, and mass gatherings. For this reason, most of us are familiar with Marin Luther King Jr. and Rosa Parks; we can recall images of the lunch counter sit-ins, police dogs, fire hoses, the massive march on Washington, the procession from Selma to Montgomery, and the bombing of black churches. Yet we know relatively little about the Southern Christian Leadership Conference, the Congress of Racial Equality, the Montgomery Improvement Association, the Fellowship of Reconciliation, the Student Nonviolent Coordinating Committee, the Women's Political Council, the Council of Federated Organizations, the Leadership Conference on Civil Rights, or the National Urban League. Along with the NAACP and an array of religious congregations, these organizations were the very core of the civil rights movement. They provided structure, education, and funding. They helped recruit new activists, organized events, trained leaders, planned strategy, and lobbied governments. Contrary to popular belief, the civil rights movement did not simply "explode" into a full-fledged social movement when Rosa Parks refused to give up her seat. Her resistance on that day was without a doubt one of the most significant symbolic acts in American history, but the social and political changes that followed were won through hundreds of other acts of resistance and thousands of hours of planning, strategizing, and sacrificing on the part of tens of thousands of activists.

The same can be said of any other social movement that succeeds in advancing positive social change. Whenever a group of people come together to publicly challenge a dominant authority over a sustained period of time, there likely exists (1) a history of shared exploitation or exclusion, (2) a coalition of supportive organizations, and (3) a dense social network of committed activists. This is true, for example, of the

U.S. labor movement that blossomed in the late 1800s and achieved economic justice for many workers, including restrictions on child labor, limits on working hours, improved wages and benefits, safety and health regulations, and a guaranteed minimum wage. It is true of the feminist movement that has fought for over a century to ensure a woman's right to vote, a guarantee of equal pay for equal work, and an end to all forms of discrimination based on gender. It is also true of the gay rights movement that advocates for the social acceptance of people with different sexual orientations, challenges the cultural presumption of heterosexuality, and works for legal equality in all social institutions. The fact that social movements tend to share a concern for civil rights and greater social equality is not a coincidence. In fact, the very historical origin of social movements coincides with the birth of modern democracy.

SOCIAL MOVEMENTS AND DEMOCRACY

Struggles for freedom, independence, and equality are not new. Ever since the first tyrant imposed his will on an unwilling population, there have been people who have fought back. Indeed, it is safe to say that much of human history is defined by relationships of domination and resistance. Slaves, in one form or another, have always struggled against the control of their masters. Serfs have resisted the domination of their lords. And poor people have regularly struggled for economic justice. But battles by subordinates to secure more equal power have not always taken the form of a social movement. As we saw in chapter 3, conformity and obedience to power are actually more common than resistance. In fact, from a historical perspective, the social movement, as I have described it above, is a relatively new form of collective action.

Most scholars believe that the first social movements developed in Europe and North America sometime in the latter half of the eighteenth century.[4] This was period of rapid social change. A growing segment of the population was learning how to read, newspapers and political pamphlets were for the first time being mass produced, and improvements in transportation were making it easier for large groups of people to meet and organize. Although England and France were still colonial powers, this was the period of European history when these two long-standing monarchies were starting to collapse. Radical ideas and "enlightened" thinking began to percolate in the heads of many intellectuals, and the revolutionary concept of "democracy" was starting to take shape.

It was within this social environment that the modern antislavery movement also started to take root. The "abolitionists," as they were called, were committed to ending the slave trade between Africa and the new colonies in North and South America. The more radical leaders also believed that every slave should be set free. This emerging group of activists would eventually form what some sociologists consider to be the world's first social movement. For the first time in history, people were (1) confronting dominant authorities using an organized coalition of groups, (2) communicating specific grievances through available media, (3) staging rallies and processions, and (4) demonstrating that a large group of committed people had the power to produce positive social change. Perhaps most importantly, the abolitionist movement came to serve as a model for all other social movements that followed. More than two hundred years after the abolitionist movement began, the tactics and strategy developed by these early advocates for democracy and equality are still being employed and were instrumental in the American civil rights movement.

Consider, for example, the effective use of the petition as a tactic for communicating collective grievances. In 1787 a small group of antislavery advocates in England formed the Society for the Abolition of the Slave Trade. In an attempt to demonstrate to the British Parliament that their cause had wide public support, they collected thousands of signatures on a single petition. It is estimated that the petition from the city of Manchester alone had eleven thousand signatures, or about two-thirds of the male population. Over the next several decades, millions of citizens from around the world would sign their names to similar antislavery petitions. In the United States, between 1831 and 1863, some three million women signed antislavery petitions that were sent to Congress. Since women were at the time excluded from political institutions and had not yet won the right to vote, these petitions also served to challenge the exclusion of women from the democratic process. [5]

The abolitionists also organized one of the first large-scale boycotts in history. Pamphlets and posters, such as the one in figure 7.1, asked consumers to boycott sugar that had been produced by slaves. These handbills were circulated throughout Great Britain, and it is estimated that in one year, some three hundred thousand families pledged to boycott slave sugar. By making effective use of the petition, boycott,

EAST INDIA SUGAR.

By six families using East India instead of West India Sugar one Slave less is required: surely to release a fellow-creature from a state of cruel bondage and misery, by so small a sacrifice, is worthy the attention of all.

N.B. The labour of one Slave produces about Ten Cwt. of Sugar annually.

J. Blackwell, Printer, Iris Office, Sheffield.

Figure 7.1. This handbill was produced in England by the Sheffield Female Anti-Slavery Society and was distributed around 1825–1833. Courtesy of the Religious Society of Friends in Britain

and print media, the abolitionists were able to expand their movement and build pressure on governments to end slavery.

It is important to recognize that the abolitionist movement contributed to the extension of democracy in two different ways. First, in their tireless struggle to extinguish slavery, many abolitionists advocated for the inherent equality of all people. It is difficult to argue that democracy is at work if specific groups of people are excluded from the political process. Accepting the humanity of blacks was the first step toward equal rights for all people. As long as blacks were believed to be biologically inferior to whites, it was relatively easy to justify slavery and limit democratic participation. On the other hand, if it could be demonstrated that blacks were intellectual equals, with the same capacity to reason, learn, and create, then arguments for second-class citizenship could be undermined. This is why the role of former slaves was so central to the success of the abolitionist movement. Olaudah Equiano, for example, who was captured at the age of ten and enslaved for more than a decade before earning his freedom, was a central figure in the British abolitionist movement. His autobiography detailing the horrors of the slave trade was widely read and immensely influential. In addition to shining a light on the cruelty of slavery, Equiano's book and public lectures revealed a former slave whose intellectual abilities were superior to that of many sophisticated white citizens.

The second way that the abolitionist movement extended democracy was by inventing a new opportunity for public participation in the political process. Boycotts, petitions, public rallies, marches, pamphlets, buttons, and other tactics of the abolitionists were for the most part available to all citizens—even those who were excluded from the formal political process. You did not have to be a man, a wealthy landowner, or a member of Parliament to become active in the movement. Women, poor people, and slaves found a democratic voice in the abolitionist movement.

Today, social movements continue to serve as a vehicle of democracy. Whenever the march toward a more democratic society is stalled, social movements often emerge to break down barriers and prod intransigent elites to get out of the way and make room for equality, justice, and shared decision making. In this way, we can see that democracy is much more than the proceedings of a legislative body or the filling out of an election ballot; it is a social process that requires collective action by all people irrespective of traditional political borders or personal boundaries. To fulfill its promise, the democratization process must therefore extend beyond official government practices to include all people in all spheres of life.

GLOBAL DEMOCRACY

Sometime early in the fall of 1999, I received an e-mail from a friend asking for help. It turns out he was working with a local labor union and wanted me to spread the word about a protest rally scheduled for November 30 in Seattle, Washington. He told me that the World Trade Organization (WTO) was scheduled to hold its international conference in Seattle and that the international business leaders who run the WTO were expected to ratify a new set of "trade agreements" that would have a major impact on the global economy. As a sociologist I was somewhat familiar with the WTO but did not consider myself to be an expert. I knew that the WTO was an undemocratic organization with immense power. I knew that the WTO was a strong advocate for "free trade" between countries, and I knew that its supporters in the Seattle area represented some of the most influential corporations in the world—Boeing, Microsoft, Starbucks, Intel, and Nike. It made sense to me that labor unions would be concerned about an organization that had so much economic power and operated outside of the democratic process. I told my friend that I would do what I could to help out.

I was not confident that I could convince too many of my colleagues at the university to attend the rally. Seattle, after all, is four hours from our campus in Oregon, and November 30 was a Tuesday—schedules would have to be changed, transportation would have to be arranged, and overnight accommodations might be necessary. Besides, November in the Pacific Northwest usually means constant rain. Nevertheless, when I raised the idea with the president of our faculty union, I was surprised to learn that the Oregon AFL-CIO (the federation representing most labor unions in the state) was already working on plans to reserve a passenger train for the trip to Seattle. It seemed that many union leaders familiar with the past practices of the WTO, and skeptical of their so-called free trade agenda, were eager to voice their concerns. The labor leaders wouldn't be allowed to sit at the table with the highly secretive leaders of the WTO, but they could certainly stand outside and share their frustration with the general public. Now I was more optimistic; if we could get fifty to one hundred union activists from Oregon to attend, there might be a couple of thousand from Washington State at the protest.

Over the next several weeks we put up posters on campus, informed other faculty about the event, and spoke to student groups about the undemocratic nature of the WTO and the implications of their plans for the global economy. Some of my colleagues were supportive but could not find the time to attend the rally. Students seemed more interested, but most showed little interest in joining the protest. On the day before the event, it was clear that only two faculty members from our campus would be on the train—the president of our union and me. About ten students had arranged to carpool up to Seattle, and they spent Monday afternoon making signs for the demonstration. It was only later that evening that my oldest son, who at the time was a student at a nearby campus, informed me that he was also driving up to Seattle with some of his friends. Although he was not part of the labor movement, he was concerned about environmental degradation and he had learned from local environmental groups that the WTO policies were threatening our ability to protect the earth. I thought to myself, if activists in the environmental movement were also organizing against the WTO, my early estimates of several thousand protesters might be low; perhaps five to six thousand would be a more accurate guess.

On the morning on November 30, when we caught our chartered Amtrak train heading north from Portland, there were well over three hundred rank-and-file union members on board. I later learned that fifteen buses had also been reserved and these too were packed with labor activists ready to demonstrate against the WTO. When we pulled into the King Street station in downtown Seattle later that morning, I was stunned by what I saw and what I heard. The atmosphere was electric, almost carnival like—union banners and colorful picket signs were on display throughout the city while marching bands and the loud thumping of distant drums set an empowering rhythmic tone. I immediately realized that my expectation of five thousand protesters was wrong; the number had to be at least fifty thousand!

I grew up in Seattle and had witnessed many political events in the city, including rallies against the Vietnam War, but I had never seen a crowd like this one. Block after block, as far as I could see, the streets and sidewalks were choked with demonstrators. But even more surprising than the colossal number of people was the diversity of the gathering. The very young mingled with the very old. I saw toddlers being pushed in strollers alongside elderly citizens in wheelchairs. Middle-class college students were marching with poor migrant farmworkers. On one corner, underneath a huge banner that read "Defend Our Forests," a group of environmental advocates wearing rain parkas was engaged in a discussion with a small congregation of Catholic nuns holding black umbrellas. The sense of solidarity among these different groups was especially remarkable. Indigenous women from Central America were flanked by longshoreman from the Seattle shipping docks. At one point a crew of brawny steelworkers locked arms with a group of lesbian activists as they marched in lockstep chanting, "Hey! Hey! Ho! Ho! The WTO has got to go!"

Our plan was to make our way through the throng of activists to Memorial Stadium, some twenty blocks away, where other labor unions were gathering for a rally. From there we would begin a march to the sight of the WTO meetings. By the time we arrived at the outdoor arena, the place was crammed with union workers from almost every profession—including machinists, carpenters, teachers, truck drivers, autoworkers, office clerks, and garment workers. The energy and solidarity among the crowd reminded me of the enthusiasm I was used to seeing at a Seahawk football game, only in this case the people did not come to be entertained by professional athletes. This massive cross-section of workers was focused on a shared economic threat—the power of global capitalism. We listened to labor leaders from across the globe share similar stories of downsizing, declining wages, and a growing frustration with the "demands" of powerful and uncompromising economic elite. It was striking how similar their concerns were.

Leroy Trotman, a union leader from the country of Barbados, represented the shared sentiment of the hour when he strode to the microphone and in a confident and powerful voice called for international unity:

> Brothers and sisters, keep the struggle going! Make sure that the leaders of the governments around the world will never forget this day—the thirtieth of November nineteen hundred and ninety nine! This demonstration is not a demonstration of United States. It is a demonstration of all working-class people all over the world—rich country, poor country, white country, black country, ALL countries.
>
> They say to us in countries like mine, Barbados, if you want jobs you have to forget trade union rights, if you want jobs you have to forget labor laws, if you want jobs you have to forget decent wages. We have said to hell with you!
>
> We believe that all people everywhere should share in the fruits of their labor, and this is why we congratulate you, we join you, and we want to fight with you to say no to the behavior of the WTO!

I did not anticipate that so many demonstrators would be drawn to Seattle from as far away as India, China, Africa, South America, and Europe. I had underestimated the growing frustration with an unjust global capitalism. I did not expect such a coordinated and cohesive reaction to the policies of the WTO. In short, I did not foresee the possible emergence of a new international social movement.

THE GLOBALIZATION MOVEMENT

In chapter 5 we saw how a new global capitalism was disrupting the lives of working people in both rich and poor countries. We also saw how global wealth was becoming increasingly concentrated in the hands of a small class of super rich capitalists. The so-called battle in Seattle was a reaction to these global trends, and many analysts now view November 30, 1999, as the symbolic birthday of a new international social movement that is currently challenging the power of multinational corporations. The WTO is not the source of every economic problem in the world; nor is it the only organization that works to advance the interests of big business. But the WTO is a powerful institution with a central role in the new global economy. For this reason, it has become a symbolic target for a range of frustrations being felt across the globe. Therefore, if we are to understand the globalization movement, we need to first begin with an examination of the WTO.

THE WORLD TRADE ORGANIZATION

If you visit the official website for the WTO, you will learn that it is headquartered in Geneva, Switzerland, and was formally instituted on January 1, 1995. You will also learn that it represents 157 "member countries" and is managed by a staff of more than six hundred employees. Perhaps most importantly, you will be told that the WTO is "the only global international organization dealing with the rules of trade between nations" and that the goal of this international body "is to help producers of goods and services, exporters, and importers conduct their business." In short, the purpose of the WTO "is to help trade flow as freely as possible."

All of this is true. The WTO is a sort of global club that focuses on economic issues. It professes to be concerned with "making life easier for all" by stimulating economic growth, promoting peace, cutting costs on products, and raising incomes of workers while encouraging good government. Clearly, these are noble ambitions, and it would be difficult to find anybody who would argue against such lofty principles. So why the protest? Why did fifty thousand people travel to Seattle to challenge an organization that was less than five years old? There are many answers to this question, but two general concerns structure the more specific complaints. First, many people think that the manner in which the WTO operates is in fact a threat to global democracy. Second, there is widespread belief that the rules established by the WTO do much more harm than good.

Let us first examine how the WTO operates. On the surface it appears to be a widely representative body. Indeed, with delegates from almost every nation in the world, it resembles, in some respects, an international congress or parliament. The problem, however, is that the so-called trade representatives are not elected by the people. For the most part, they are appointed by their government leaders, and many of these leaders rule undemocratic governments. As a result, the voices on the WTO rarely speak to the concerns of workers, peasants, and poor people that form the vast majority of the world's population. What we find instead is that the concerns of the powerful multinational corporations are given priority, and the leaders of the world's wealthiest economies end up having the most influence.

Another problem is that when the representatives get together to establish the international rules of trade and commerce, they do so behind closed doors, without the transparency and public participation that characterizes a free and open democratic system. This element of secrecy is most insidious when disagreements between countries arise. When this happens, three trade officials are selected to serve as temporary judges with the authority to rule on disputes between nations on matters of international trade law.[6] The power of this small group cannot be overstated. Unlike other international organizations, the WTO has the ability to enforce its decisions. Nations that violate the rules of the WTO can face harsh financial penalties and trade sanctions severe enough to send a nation's economy into a tailspin. Thus, even if a ruling of the WTO contradicts the law of a democratic government, the "offending" nation is coerced into compliance.

For example, in 1994 the U.S. government amended the Clean Air Act to require foreign gasoline refiners to improve the quality of their gas before it could be used in the United States. The intent of the law was to reduce harmful emissions present in imported gasoline. But when the WTO ruled in 1996 that this was a violation of free trade agreements, the United States was forced to back down and had to allow the importing of gas that produces greater air pollution. As this case illustrates, the enforcement of a WTO rule does not necessarily lead to a better world. More importantly, when local laws can be over-ridden by a small international panel, democracy is diminished.

The WTO operates under the guiding philosophy that "free trade" will make the world a better place. Those who advocate for radical free trade or "neoliberalism" make the assumption that restrictions on what can be sold in the world marketplace will be bad for the global economy. However, the evidence has not supported this faith in an unbridled and undemocratic capitalism.[7] As we saw in chapter 5, an unrestricted global economy leads to a concentration of wealth rather than a fair and equitable distribution of resources. When governments cannot discriminate against how products are made or harvested, it is harder to enforce local and national laws that are designed to protect the environment, secure worker rights, and guard consumer safety.

We can see evidence of this, for example, in a 2006 ruling by the WTO that addressed food safety. Today, most countries in Europe have laws that ban the sale of food that has been produced using "genetically modified organisms" (GMOs). The concern is that GMOs are a potential threat to biodiversity and may, when used under certain conditions, be a health hazard. Nevertheless, a WTO tribunal ruled that the European ban on GMO violates WTO-established trade rules. While this judgment clearly contradicts the will of the European citizenry, it supports the economic interests of multinational agribusiness corporations such as Monsanto, DuPont, and Dow Chemical.

The WTO bias in favor of big business is also evident in a 2005 ruling. The issue in this particular case was gambling. In the United States a number of governmental bodies have enacted laws that restrict the operation of gambling on the Internet. But because these controls of online betting are not in the interest of the international gaming industry, their business leaders brought the issue before the WTO. The small Caribbean island of Antigua, where many gambling companies locate their offices, argued that their free trade was being restricted—and the tribunal agreed. The final verdict asserted that the U.S. laws were discriminatory and inconsistent with the rules of the WTO. The fact that the U.S. government had legally enacted the restrictions on gambling did not matter.

As was noted already, the WTO is not the only international organization designed to advance the interests of multinational corporations. The World Bank and the International Monetary Fund (IMF) are also powerful institutions that seek to change social and economic policies around the world in support of the "free trade" agenda. Space does not allow for a comprehensive review of these other institutions, but it is important to know that protesters in Seattle were also frustrated by the collaboration among the WTO, the IMF, and the World Bank. All three organizations represent the goals of elite capitalists who seek to dominate the global economy by extending their right to profit without restraint. This is why countries are being pressured to privatize public health and retirement systems. This is why countries are being told that they can't limit foreign ownership of their natural resources. And this is why citizens concerned about economic democracy are fighting back.

PROTECTING POWER

The mass of protesters who joined in Seattle to confront the undemocratic proceedings of the WTO posed a threat to the growing power of multinational corporations. They challenged the dominant "free trade" mantra of the economic elites and advocated an alternative plan that emphasized "fair trade." This was a very public battle over ideas and social policy that the WTO wanted to avoid. And when hundreds of young people sat down, locked arms, and blocked entrances to buildings, business as usual was disrupted. History shows us that democratic social movements do not achieve victory without a fight. As abolitionist Frederick Douglass correctly recognized 150 years ago, "If there is no struggle, there is no progress." This was certainly the case in Seattle on November 30, 1999. Faced with an unexpected uprising from fifty thousand citizens, the powerful did not change course; they simply fought back.

By midmorning, police in full riot gear were moving into downtown Seattle. They were escorted by armored vehicles with cannons that fired concussion grenades and canisters of CS gas. The officers carried truncheons and rifles equipped with plastic bullets. The following account from an eyewitness provides a sense of what followed:

> In one scene I witnessed this morning (at 8th Ave. and Seneca), police who had been standing behind a blockade line began marching in lockstep toward the line, swinging their batons forward, and when they reached the line they began striking the (nonviolent, seated) protestors repeatedly in the back. Then they ripped off the protestors' gas masks, and sprayed pepper spray at point-blank range into their eyes repeatedly. After spraying, they rubbed the protestors' eyes and pushed their fingers around on their lips to aggravate the effect of the spray. And after all THIS, they began striking them again with batons. . . . The police then were able to break up the line, and the protestors retreated to the steps of a nearby church for medical assistance. [8]

The ensuing crackdown on peaceful protesters and others committed to civil disobedience escalated when the mayor declared a state of emergency and called in the National Guard. Over the next two days, hundreds of people were physically injured and had to be treated for damage to their eyes and for wounds caused by plastic bullets. Hundreds more were indiscriminately rounded up, handcuffed, placed on commandeered city buses, and transported to a giant airplane hanger that served as a temporary jail. Perhaps most disturbing of all, however, was the unilateral suspension of civil rights ordered by those in power.

A curfew of 5:00 p.m. was enforced for downtown Seattle, and an official "no protest" zone was established. Anyone seen carrying a sign, distributing leaflets, or even wearing a button would be arrested. Even some journalists were caught in the military dragnet. A correspondent for the *Seattle Post-Intelligencer* reported that "three Seattle police officers slammed me to the pavement, handcuffed me, and threw me into the van. I was charged with failing to disperse even though I showed them reporter's credentials and repeatedly said I was just covering a story."[9] Most of the television media focused their attention on a handful of young people who attacked storefront symbols of corporate greed—Nike Town, McDonald's, Starbucks, and so on. There was very little coverage of the fact that the rights of citizens were violated in a desperate attempt to preserve a meeting of the WTO. It took seven years of litigation, but a federal jury eventually ruled that the city of Seattle was liable for the unlawful arrests of the WTO protesters. A settlement of $1 million was divided among the hundreds who brought suit against the city.

The question remains, however, why did the government leaders in the city of Seattle and the state of Washington order an illegal repression of protesters? At one level this is a psychological question that requires knowledge of the reasoning employed by those in power. But we can also examine this question more objectively if we understand the protest in terms of its wider history and social context. The WTO summit was a gathering of some of the most powerful people in the world, including then-president Bill Clinton. Clinton and most of the other elites were very strong and vocal supporters of the so-called free trade agenda advocated by the WTO. In this sense, the mass demonstration not only threatened the meeting of the WTO; it also threatened the economic agenda of key political leaders, as well as the financial interests of global corporations. It is one thing to hold a rally in support of, say, immigrant rights, or to demonstrate against the death penalty, but to challenge the capitalist premise of the global economy is to confront the very center of global power. The crackdown by those in control of the military and police is usually proportionate to the power and economic interest at stake.

In the end the WTO meetings were suspended, as were the civil rights of hundreds of demonstrators. Downtown Seattle eventually got back to its ordinary business, and the protesters eventually returned to their everyday lives. But the issue of who controls the global economy remained unresolved. Over the next decade dozens of mass protests similar to the battle in Seattle were organized across the globe. Some of these were directed at the WTO, while others focused on related institutions and groups controlling the direction of international trade policy. Below is a partial list of the protest locations, dates, and the estimated size of the crowds[10]:

November 30, 1999	Seattle, Washington	50,000
April 16, 2000	Washington, D.C.	20,000
September 11, 2000	Melbourne, Australia	30,000
September 26, 2000	Prague, Czechoslovakia	15,000
April 20, 2001	Quebec, Canada	30,000
June 25, 2001	Barcelona, Spain	20,000
July 20, 2001	Genoa, Italy	300,000
April 20, 2002	Washington, D.C.	70,000
September 14, 2003	Cancun, Mexico	10,000
November 20, 2003	Miami, Florida	15,000
November 23, 2004	Santiago, Chile	20,000
April 29, 2004	Warsaw, Poland	3,500
December 13, 2005	Hong Kong, China	10,000
November 18, 2006	Melbourne, Australia	3,000
June 2, 2007	Rostock, Germany	50,000
March 28, 2009	London, England	35,000

After the protest in Seattle, police and military became ever-more vigilant and sophisticated in their techniques for controlling demonstrators. They have deployed more troops, erected fences around meeting locations, infiltrated movement organizations, and cordoned off blocks of host cities to prevent contact between citizens and economic elites. Still, tens of thousands of people continue to be arrested, hundreds have been injured, and a small number have even been killed.

It is important to emphasize, however, that the globalization movement is not defined simply by the size and number of public demonstrations. Like most other modern social movements, the globalization movement is working diligently to extend democracy. This can be seen in the thousands of organizations across the globe where members are cooperating to advance a democratically controlled economy, one where a living wage, public health, respect for human dignity, and protection of the environment form a shared vision. For this reason it is wrong to characterize the globalization movement as antiglobalization; such an oversimplified misrepresentation is often used to discredit activists and protesters as naive and unrealistic. In fact, the globalization movement supports greater global communication and advocates for increasing international solidarity. The difference is between those who push a top-down "globalization from above" and those who advocate for a grassroots "globalization from below."[11]

The positive vision of a more egalitarian globalization process has been well represented at an annual international gathering of activists and organizations committed to globalization from below known as the World Social Forum (WSF). The very first WSF was held in 2001 in Porto Alegre, Brazil. At this historic assembly about eleven thousand participants from around the world spent several days sharing local and regional experiences, discussing common goals, and debating movement strategy. At the 2005 WSF there were more than 150,000 registered participants attending workshops, listening to presentations, and engaging in democratic deliberation. Since then, the WSF has adopted a more polycentric approach, with smaller simultaneous gatherings in multiple cities around the globe. What makes the WSF unique is that participants are not allowed to represent political parties or military institutions; only nongovernmental organizations (NGOs) and unaffiliated individuals are invited.

According to its Charter Principles,

> The World Social Forum seeks to strengthen and create new national and international links among organizations and movements of society that, in both public and private life, will increase the capacity for nonviolent social resistance to the process of dehumanization the world is undergoing. . . . The alternatives proposed at the World Social Forum stand in opposition to a process of globalization commanded by the large multinational corporations and by the governments and international institutions at the service of those corporations' interests, with the complicity of national governments. They are designed to ensure that globalization in solidarity will prevail as a new stage in world history. This will respect universal human rights and those of all citizens—men and women—of all nations and the environment and will rest on democratic international systems and institutions at the service of social justice, equality, and the sovereignty of peoples.

This vision of international solidarity might seem unrealistic and naively impractical, but every social movement is guided by a set of ideal principles and a collective belief that a better world is possible. The shared values of democracy, social justice, equality, and human dignity do not cause revolutions or instigate positive social change on their own. Real change happens when people organize for collective action and engage in the hard work of remaking social institutions. But when ideal principles are widely shared, our common humanity is more easily recognized, and we are better able to find ways around traditional barriers associated with differences in language, culture, and religion. This is what happened in 2011 as activists in the global democracy movement inspired each other with acts of resistance and collective solidarity.

GLOBAL SOLIDARITY

In chapter 6 we learned how the tragic suicide of Mohamed Bouazizi helped inspire a revolution in Tunisia and trigger a series of uprisings throughout North Africa and the Middle East. One of the most visually dramatic episodes of the Arab Spring was the mass occupation of Tahrir Square in Cairo, Egypt. The world watched in awe on January 25, 2011, as thousands of citizens flooded into Egypt's capital city and risked their lives to protest the dictatorship of Hosni Mubarak. Each day the occupation of the square grew in size in the face of violent attacks by the military and secret police. And seventeen days after the occupation began, Mubarak was ousted from power, marking the first steps on a path toward democratic rule.

On the other side of the world, in another capital city, a group of frustrated graduate students took note. They were not living under the rule of a dictator, but they were, nevertheless, discouraged by the actions of their political leaders. This was Madison, Wisconsin, and newly elected governor Scott Walker, along with his fellow Republican legislators, were about to pass a bill that would strip public labor unions of their right to engage in collective bargaining. The graduate students were members of the Teaching Assistants Association at the University of Wisconsin, and if the proposed law were to pass, the TAs would no longer have a legal right to negotiate with their bosses over the conditions of their work. As the students saw it, democracy was taking a step backwards, and they were not prepared to let this happen without a fight.

Just three days after the Egyptian people succeeded in their occupation of Tahrir Square, the teaching assistants organized their own march on the Wisconsin State Capitol Building. On day 1, about one thousand protesters participated—almost all were students—but the turnout was larger than expected, and the action inspired other public unions to join in. On the second day, thirteen thousand teachers, firefighters, police officers, nurses, and other public employees joined the students and swarmed into the capitol building where many of them set up camp for the night. By day 3, the crowd had attracted national media attention as their ranks swelled to twenty thousand, then twenty-five thousand, and then forty thousand, and by day 6 the mass protest was estimated to be sixty-eight thousand strong! Now the whole world was watching, including the Egyptians, many of whom voiced their support for the Wisconsin uprising. Maor Eletrebi, one of the leaders of the Egyptian revolution, sent a letter of solidarity to the Wisconsin union members and their supporters. It read, in part, "To Our Friends in Madison, Wisconsin: I wish you could see firsthand the change we have made here. Justice is beautiful, but justice is never free. The beauty of Tahrir Square you can have everywhere, on any corner, in any city, or in your heart. So hold on tightly and don't let go." [12]

Shortly after the occupations of Madison and Cairo, another prodemocracy occupation began to take shape. This new protest was initiated by people who were frustrated with the growing influence of big money in American politics. In a true democracy, rich people should not have any more influence in government than poor people. Ideally, the young student, unemployed construction worker, retired homemaker, or small business owner should have as much weight in politics as the wealthy elites who run big corporations, control the investment banks, lead the military, and manage our universities. While most Americans recognize that this is not the case, the typical citizen feels incapable of changing the system. Nevertheless, in the fall of 2011, a small group of citizens in New York City, inspired by the Arab Spring and the Wisconsin demonstrations, also decided to take action.

It began with the following challenge posted on the website of a small prodemocracy magazine:

Are you ready for a Tahrir moment?
On Sept 17, flood into lower Manhattan,

set up tents, kitchens, peaceful barricades and
Occupy Wall Street. [13]

Wall Street is the home of the New York Stock Exchange; it is the
location of the largest investment banks in the world; and it is considered the financial center of global capitalism. In the eyes of many, Wall
Street is also a symbol of excess wealth and unrestrained power. By
occupying Wall Street the protesters hoped to focus attention on the
inequities inherent in the U.S. political-economic system. The initial
organizers had low expectations but were encouraged when several
hundred people showed up to participate on the first day. Police barri-
caded Wall Street itself, so the group set up camp at nearby Zuccotti
Park. In the days and weeks that followed, the encampment and associated protest rallies grew to over thirty thousand. Soon a new rallying
cry spread across the country: "We are the 99%!"—a reference to the
fact that the wealthiest 1 percent of the nation controls an enormously
disproportionate share of wealth and power. By early October, hundreds of thousands of citizens were staging similar occupations in every major city in the United States, including Washington, D.C., Boston,
Philadelphia, Atlanta, Memphis, Chicago, Denver, Cincinnati, Los Angeles, San Francisco, Portland, and Seattle. Even small towns like
McAllen, Texas; Mosier, Oregon; and West Plains, Missouri, were
participating. And on October 15, solidarity rallies were held in more
than nine hundred cities across the globe. In Spain, where the economy
was particularly depressed, protesters numbered five hundred thousand
in Madrid and four hundred thousand in Barcelona.

As I write these words in the fall of 2012, the protesters in Madison
have disbanded and the occupiers of Zuccotti Park have been dispersed.
Scott Walker is still governor of Wisconsin; massive cuts to public
services are being planned for Spain; and the wealthiest 1 percent still
dominates politics in the United States. But it is still too early in the
global democracy movement to gauge its success. For this reason we
should not be too eager to dismiss its democratic objectives, nor should
we deride its optimistic claim that "another world is possible." After
all, almost two hundred years separated the first victories of the abolitionist movement and the advances resulting from the American civil
rights movement. Democratic progress can be slow, but it would be
wrong to underestimate the power of collective action; indeed, history
demonstrates that the journey to social justice has always been escorted

by a community of committed activists empowered by the energy of a social movement.

Conclusion

Sociology is the study of social life, social change, and the social causes and consequences of human behavior.

—American Sociological Association

The sociological perspective is more like a demon that possesses one, that drives one compellingly, again and again, to the questions that are its own. An introduction to sociology is, therefore, an invitation to a very special kind of passion.

—Peter L. Berger [1]

Sociology is both an academic discipline and a perspective. As an academic discipline, sociology is relatively easy to recognize and describe. It is a scientific subject area, a body of knowledge with theories and findings, a set of courses listed in a college catalog, book titles on a library shelf, and the day-to-day work of scientists and professors. But as a perspective, sociology is less formal, more subjective, and less easily defined. Sociology in this second sense is an orientation or point of view that provides a unique way of perceiving and understanding the world around us. It is a perspective that directs our attention away from the isolated individual and toward groups, institutions, and the web of social connections that we call society.

For many people the sociological perspective is a difficult viewpoint to adopt. It often goes against well-established assumptions regarding human nature and personal identity. Yet, for the very same reason, sociology can become a new and exciting approach—even a passion. The overarching goal of this book has been to develop and enhance the adoption of sociology as a perspective and to stoke the embers of a smoldering passion.

About five hundred years ago almost every educated European assumed that the earth was the center of our planetary system. All of the visible planets and the sun were thought to be in orbit around the earth. This geocentric perspective seemed obvious and indisputable to most. After all, one need only look into the sky to "see" that as the earth remained stationary, the sun would "rise" and "set" along with the moon and other distant stars. Moreover, the Bible was clear on the matter, and the church leaders were adamant that any point of view that claimed otherwise was heresy. It took many years, but eventually the mathematical and scientific evidence proved overwhelming, and today it is difficult to find an educated person anywhere in the world who does not accept the sun as the center of our planetary system. We may still say that sun "rises" and "sets," but we know it is the earth that is spinning on its axis and revolving around the sun. This heliocentric perspective of the cosmos did not change the movement of heavenly bodies; it simply changed our perception of how the earth, moon, sun, and stars are related to each other.

Sociological theories and evidence offer similar challenges to conventional ways of explaining human social behavior. A sociological perspective represents a shift in perception away from the dominant individualistic point of view and toward an orientation that sees social relationships and social forces as primary and fundamental. It is a point of view that asks us to step back from ourselves and observe human interaction from a distance, to ponder our dependence on others, and to be informed by this new gaze. When astronaut Neil Armstrong was asked about his experience of walking on the moon, he said, "It suddenly struck me that that tiny pea, pretty and blue, was the Earth. I put up my thumb and shut one eye, and my thumb blotted out the planet Earth. I didn't feel like a giant. I felt very, very small." In some ways, a sociological perspective can be similarly humbling.

Throughout this book we have identified some of the diverse social forces that have the power to limit and shape our individual life choices. While it may be true that social forces rarely have complete control over us, it also true that no single individual is ever completely "free to choose." In fact, we are almost always faced with a limited set of life options, and, more often than not, these options are determined by social forces outside of our own personal control. The fact that we may not recognize or perceive these forces does not alter their power.

From the moment we take in our first breath to the day we exhale for the last time, our life is inextricably linked to the lives of others. For infants this social interdependence is obvious and easily recognized, but as we mature and become more confident in our ability to fend for ourselves, there is a tendency to exaggerate individual power and to adopt a perspective that emphasizes personal autonomy, self-reliance, and self-determination. This seems to be especially true in American society where the myth of individualism is a deeply held cultural belief. To adopt a sociological perspective is to swim against this commanding cultural current. It is a task that requires intellectual persistence and an open mind. Sociology is not simply an alternative ideology. It is not based on faith, and it does not require the devout commitment of true believers. Like all other scientific disciplines, sociology assumes a critical and skeptical orientation and demands systematic investigations and empirical evidence in support of its truth claims.

In this book we have not sought to review the complete body of evidence in support of the sociological perspective; this would be a daunting task for any single volume. Rather, we have focused on some compelling examples in an attempt to illustrate some of the predominant social forces that shape our lives in contemporary society.

- We reviewed the treatment of so-called witches and missing links to demonstrate how our definition of personhood has changed over time in a manner that usually reflects the interests of those with power.
- We explored the deep and far-reaching influence of symbolic communication and showed how seemingly private processes of thinking and feeling are, in fact, structured by social forces.
- We examined research on groups and group membership and saw how easy it is to produce dramatic acts of conformity that often contradict personal expectations and intentions.
- We looked at the relationship between family and social class and saw how cultural capital functions as a resource that advantages some families and hinders others.
- We investigated the global reach of a modern capitalism, the economic connections among people on opposite sides of the world, and the sometimes devastating changes that globalization has brought to individuals and communities across the planet.

- We investigated how mass media promote violence and negative cultural stereotypes, while also serving as an effective tool for resisting tyranny.
- We analyzed the power of collective action and reviewed examples of how triumphant social movements have shaped social policy and moved governments toward more egalitarian and democratic practices.

In adopting a sociological perspective, we acknowledge the power of these social forces and we question social policies and theories of human behavior that assert the primacy of individual power. In short, when we adopt a sociological perspective, we come to appreciate the complex web of social relationships in which we are all connected.

Finally, a sociological orientation warns against simple explanations that fail to consider the complexity of social life. Thus, when contemplating the pervasive influence of social forces, it can be tempting to think of society as a giant puppet master that secretly controls our movements from behind a curtain. This would be a mistake. Social forces do not have complete control over our behavior, and society does not exist independent of our own actions. We inherit social conditions from generations before us, but these conditions are never permanent. The patterns of social action that produce harm, reinforce economic inequality, and sustain discrimination can be altered. Removing the blinders of individualism is a first step toward achieving this change.

Notes

INTRODUCTION

1. Excerpt from Abraham Lincoln's debate with Stephen A. Douglas at Charleston, Illinois, September 18, 1858.

2. Dr. Pedro A. Ynterian, Great Ape Project board member, December 14, 2006, press release, http://www.greatapeproject.org/news.php.

3. "Spanish Parliament Approves Human Rights for Apes," *Guardian*, June 26, 2008.

4. Ironically, the scientist who argued for the patent was attempting to prevent other scientists from engaging in such experimentation.

5. See, for example, Joseph Veroff, Elizabeth Douvan, and Richard Kulka, *The Inner American: A Self-Portrait from 1957 to 1976* (New York: Basic Books, 1981); Jean M. Twenge, Emodish M. Abebe, and W. Keith Campbell, "Fitting In or Standing Out: Trends in American Parents' Choices for Children's Names, 1880–2007," *Social Psychology and Personality Science* 1 (2010): 19–25; and Daphna Oyserman, Heather M. Coon, and Markus Kemmelmeir, "Rethinking Individualism and Collectivism: Evaluation of Theoretical Assumptions and Meta-Analysis," *Psychological Bulletin* 128, no. 1 (2002): 3–72.

6. For a comprehensive historical analysis of the origin of individualism, see Raymond Martin and John Barresi, *The Rise and Fall of Soul and Self: An Intellectual History of Personal Identity* (New York: Columbia University Press, 2006), and Jerrold Seigel, *The Idea of Self: Thought and Experience in Western Europe since the Seventeenth Century* (Cambridge: Cambridge University Press, 2005).

7. From "Democracy in America," trans. Arthur Goldhammer, vol. 2, part 2, chap. 2 (New York: Library of America, 2004 [1856]), 585.

8. George Orwell, *1984* (Fairfield, IA: 1st World Library, 2004), 89.

9. C. Wright Mills, *The Sociological Imagination* (New York: Oxford University Press, 2000 [1959]).

10. Karl Marx, *The Eighteenth Brumaire of Louis Bonaparte* (Rockville, MD: Wildside Press, 2008 [1852]), 15.

1. INDIVIDUALISM

1. Emile Durkheim, *Selected Writings*, ed. Anthony Giddens (Cambridge: Cambridge University Press, 1972), 113. Emile Durkheim (1858–1917) was one of the early founders of academic sociology.

2. This account of Ted Kaczynski's life relies heavily on Alston Chase's *Harvard Unabomber: The Education of an American Terrorist* (New York: Norton, 2003). Unless otherwise noted, all quotations are taken from this source.

3. See especially Robert N. Bellah, Richard Madsen, William M. Sullivan, Ann Swidler, and Steven M. Tipton, *Habits of the Heart: Individualism and Commitment in American Life* (Berkeley: University of California Press, 1985); Andrie Kusserow, *American Individualisms: Child Rearing and Social Class in Three Neighborhoods* (New York: Palgrave MacMillan, 2004); and Charles Lemert and Anthony Elliot, *Deadly Worlds: The Emotional Costs of Globalization* (Lanham, MD: Rowman & Littlefield, 1986).

4. For an excellent overview, see Steven Lukes, *Individualism* (New York: Harper & Row, 1973).

5. Kaczynski's life also demonstrates in numerous ways that it is impossible to become a complete individualist. Even though he isolated himself physically from others, he was still engaged in attempts to remake the social world through acts of terror. One might even argue that he desired notoriety, which itself reflects a level of social engagement.

6. These findings are taken from the World Values Survey conducted by a network of international social scientists (http://www.worldvaluessurvey.org/). We should interpret these results with some caution. Differences between cultures are complex and cannot be easily reduced to answers on a questionnaire. This may be especially true for countries like Nigeria, which encompasses many different ethnic groups and includes over 250 different language communities within its borders.

7. See, for example, Ian Watt, *Myths of Modern Individualism: Faust, Don Quixote, Don Juan, Robinson Crusoe* (Cambridge: Cambridge University Press, 1996). But even before the first novels were written, the celebration of a heroic individual can be found two thousand years earlier in ancient Greek mythology. Homer's epic poems the *Iliad* and the *Odyssey*, for example, have themes and characters that continue to be reflected in popular culture.

8. For an excellent introductory overview of contemporary capitalism, see Michael D. Yates, *Naming the System: Inequality and Work in the Global Economy* (New York: Monthly Review Press, 2003). For a more specific treatment of the relationship between capitalism and individualism, see Michael Perelman, *Manufacturing Discontent: The Trap of Individualism in Corporate Society* (London: Pluto Press, 2005).

9. Milton Friedman and Rose Friedman, *Free to Choose* (New York: Harcourt, 1980), 246.

10. From an interview by Geoffrey Norman published in *Playboy* magazine, February 1973.

11. Athens was the strongest and most influential Greek city-state that flourished between 400 and 500 BC.

12. From the April 6, 1859, Letter to Henry Pierce.

13. Jefferson Davis's Second Inaugural Address, February 22, 1862.

14. Excerpt from letter written while incarcerated in the Birmingham, Alabama, jail, April 16, 1963.

15. Excerpt from speech delivered at Southeastern Fairgrounds, Atlanta, Georgia, July 4, 1964.

16. Excerpt from a speech to the Republican National Convention, September 2, 2004.

17. Excerpt from videotape broadcast on Al Jazeera TV as reported by BBC and CNN, October 29, 2004.

18. The original distinction between positive and negative liberty can be traced back to the philosopher Immanuel Kant (1724–1804), but it was first systematically developed by philosopher Isaiah Berlin (1909–1997).

19. Excerpt from address to the Southern Christian Leadership Conference on August 16, 1967.

20. A version of this story was often told by Saul Alinsky (1909–1972), one of the founders of modern-day community organizing.

21. Excerpt from Ted Kaczynski's manifesto.

22. The findings reported here are taken from Robert D. Putnam's research on social capital. See especially his book *Bowling Alone: The Collapse and Revival of American Community* (New York: Simon & Schuster, 2000).

23. M. McPherson, L. Smith-Lovin, and M. E. Brahears, "Social Isolation in America: Changes in Core Discussion Networks over Two Decades," *American Sociological Review* 71 (2006): 353–75.

24. As reported by Chase in *Harvard Unabomber*.

2. BECOMING A PERSON

1. For historical accounts of witch hunts in Europe and North America, see Brian P. Levack, *The Witch-Hunt in Early Modern Europe* (London: Longman, 1987); and Paul Boyer and Stephen Nissenbaum, *Salem Possessed: The Social Origins of Witchcraft* (Cambridge, MA: Harvard University Press, 1974). Much of the information presented here comes from these sources as well as the original transcripts of the Salem witch trials.

2. This was a derogatory term often used by English Protestants to refer to Catholics. It reflects a strongly held sentiment that the pope was leading a corrupt and illegitimate wing of Christianity.

3. For a very influential analysis of the wider sociological implications of the Puritan doctrine of predestination, see Max Weber's *Protestant Ethic and the Spirit of Capitalism* (Chemsford, MA: Courier Dover Publications, 2003).

4. Excerpt from court proceedings, as quoted by Boyer and Nissenbaum, *Salem Possessed*, 192.

5. Kai T. Erikson, *Wayward Puritans: A Study in the Sociology of Deviance* (New York: Wiley, 1966).

6. Carol F. Karlson, *The Devil in the Shape of a Woman* (New York: Norton, 1987).

7. As quoted by Elizabeth Ewen and Stuart Ewen in *Typecasting: On the Arts and Sciences of Human Inequality* (New York: Seven Stories Press, 2006). This source provides an excellent historical interpretation of the eugenics movement and other sociological forces and cultural images linked to the legitimation of inequality. For a powerful video documentary that covers similar themes in a different case, see *The Life and Times of Sara Baartman* (New York: Icarus/First Run Films, 1998).

8. Title 18 of the U.S. Code, Section 1464 (18 U.S.C. § 1464).

9. We typically refer to the use of hand symbols as "sign language," but this is the more conventional use of the term sign. Sign language is actually the use of hand *symbols* and is therefore no different from oral language.

10. For an engaging and original examination of cognition from a sociological perspective, see Eviatar Zerubavel's book *Social Mindscapes: An Invitation to Cognitive Sociology* (Cambridge, MA: Harvard University Press, 1997).

11. For an excellent introductory overview of this research, see *The Monitor on Psychology* 37, no. 2 (February 2006).

12. For details on this study, see M. Morris and K. Peng, "Culture and Cause: American and Chinese Attributions for Social and Physical Events," *Journal of Personality and Social Psychology* 67 (1994): 949–71. Similar cross-cultural differences are summarized in David Matsumoto, ed., *Handbook of Cross-Cultural Psychology* (Oxford: Oxford University Press, 2000).

13. For a very comprehensive critique of research used to support group differences in intelligence, see Stephen Jay Gould, *The Mismeasure of Man* (New York: Norton, 1981).

14. For an excellent historical analysis of IQ testing and its relationship to the eugenics movement, see Ewen and Ewen, *Typecasting*.

15. See Stanley Schacter and Jerome Singer, "Cognitive, Social, and Physiological Determinants of Emotional States," *Psychological Review* 69 (1962): 379–99.

16. Allen C. Smith III and Sherryl Kleinman, "Managing Emotions in Medical School: Students' Contacts with the Living and the Dead," *Social Psychology Quarterly* 52, no. 1 (1989): 56–69.

17. Arlie Russell Hochschild, *The Managed Heart: Commercialization of Human Feeling* (Berkeley: University of California Press, 1983).

18. For a more extensive analysis of edgework, see Stephen Lyng, ed., *Edgework: The Sociology of Risk Taking* (New York: Routledge, 2005).

19. See Oyeronke Oyewumi, *The Invention of Women: Making an African Sense of Western Gender Discourses* (Minneapolis: University of Minnesota Press, 1997).

20. See Noel Ignatiev, *How the Irish Became White* (New York: Routledge, 1995).

3. CONFORMITY AND DISOBEDIENCE

1. C. S. Lewis (1898–1963) was an author, English professor, and devout Christian.

2. Mary Wollstonecraft (1759–1797) was a philosopher and strong advocate for women's rights.

3. Segments of the actual video footage can be viewed online at YouTube.com. Parts were also shown on the ABC News show *Primetime*. My description of the event relies on the videotape recording, court testimony, and several media reports.

4. For a recent review and replication of the Milgram experiment, see Jerry M. Burger, "Replicating Milgram: Would People Still Obey Today?" *American Psychologist* 64, no. 1 (2009): 1–11.

5. These quotations are taken from two historical documents: *Principles and Purposes of the KKK* and *The Klansman's Manual*, 1924. Both are archived in the Michigan State University Collection.

6. This is not his real name. The pseudonym is used to protect privacy.

7. It is important to stress that, like the Milgram experiment, certain aspects of this research methodology are considered unethical by today's research standards.

8. From Muzafer Sherif, O. J. Harvey, B. Jack White, William R. Hood, and Carolyn W. Sherif, *Intergroup Conflict and Cooperation: The Robbers Cave Experiment* (Norman: University of Oklahoma Book Exchange, 1954/1961).

9. This is not his real name.

10. For details, see Ronald Inglehart, Mansoor Moaddel, and Mark Tessler, "Xenophobia and In-Group Solidarity in Iraq: A Natural Experiment on the Impact of Insecurity," *Perspectives on Politics* 4, no. 3 (2006): 495–505.

4. FAMILY MATTERS

1. Annette Lareau, *Unequal Childhoods: Class, Race, and Family Life* (Berkeley: University of California Press, 2003). For a related study, see Andrie Kusserow, *American Individualisms: Child Rearing and Social Class in Three Neighborhoods* (New York: Palgrave Macmillan, 2004).

2. See, for example, Emily Beller and Michael Hout, "Intergenerational Social Mobility: The United States in Comparative Perspective," *Future of Children* 16, no. 2 (2006): 19–36.

3. Stanley Aronowitz, *How Class Works: Power and Social Movement* (New Haven, CT: Yale University Press, 2004), 31.

4. For a more detailed account, see Stephen R. Haynes, *Noah's Curse: The Biblical Justification of American Slavery* (Oxford: Oxford University Press, 2002).

5. Larry R. Morrison, "Religious Defense of American Slavery before 1830," *Journal of Religious Thought* 37, no. 2 (1981): 16–29.

6. For a detailed overview of wealth distribution in the United States, see Lisa A. Keister, *Getting Rich: A Study of Wealth Mobility in America* (Cambridge: Cambridge University Press, 2005). For an excellent analysis of the wealthiest Americans as a social class, see G. William Domhoff, *Who Rules America? Power, Politics, and Social Change*, 6th ed. (New York: McGraw-Hill, 2009).

7. Robert Rosenthal and Lenore Jacobson, *Pygmalion in the Classroom* (New York: Holt, Rinehart & Winston, 1968).

8. Richard J. Herrnstein and Charles Murray exhibited this particular myth of individualism in their book *The Bell Curve: Intelligence and Class Structure in American Life* (New York: Free Press, 1994). The weak evidence and poor data analyses used to support their argument was expertly exposed by a wide range of scholars. See, for example, Russell Jacoby and Naomi Glauberman, eds., *The Bell Curve Debate* (New York: Three Rivers Press, 1995).

9. For an excellent introductory analysis of inequality that employs this same game metaphor, see Michael Schwalbe, *Rigging the Game: How Inequality Is Reproduced in Everyday Life* (Oxford: Oxford University Press, 2007).

10. See, for example, *Class and Conformity: A Study in Values* (Homewood, IL: Dorsey Press, 1969); *Work and Personality: An Inquiry into the Impact of Social Stratification* (with Carmi Schooler) (Norwood, NJ: Ablex, 1983); *Change and Stability: A Cross-National Analysis of Social Structure and Personality* (Boulder, CO: Paradigm, 2006).

11. From Nick Bromell, "Scooter Libby and Me," *American Scholar*, January 16, 2007. WASP is an acronym for white, Anglo-Saxon, and Protestant—the characteristics that define most of the upper class in America.

5. GLOBALIZATION

1. Vandana Shiva (born 1952) is an internationally recognized philosopher and environmental activist.

2. The information about Tim Dewey and his family is from Louis Uchitelle, *The Disposable American: Layoffs and Their Consequences* (New York: Vintage, 2007).

3. Joseph Stiglitz, "Interpreting the Causes of the Great Recession of 2008," lecture prepared for the Eighth BIS Annual Conference, Basel, Switzerland, June, 25–26 2009.

4. Stiglitz, "Interpreting the Causes."

5. David Himmelstein, Deborah Thorne, Elizabeth Warren, and Steffie Woolhandler, "Medical Bankruptcy in the United States, 2007: Results of a National Study," *American Journal of Medicine* 122, no. 8 (August 2009): 741–46.

6. Richard Sennett, *The Corrosion of Character: The Personal Consequences of Work in the New Capitalism* (New York: Norton, 1998), 26–27.

7. See, for example, Sarah Moore, Leon Grunberg, Richard Anderson-Connolly, and Edward S. Greenberg, "Physical and Mental Health Effects of Surviving Layoffs: A Longitudinal Examination," Working Paper, Institute of Behavioral Science and Research Program on Political and Economic Change, University of Colorado, Boulder, November 2003.

8. T. A. Blakely, S. C. D. Collings, and J. Atkinson, "Unemployment and Suicide: Evidence for a Causal Association?" *Journal of Epidemiology and Community Health* 57 (2003): 594–60.

9. Avner Ahituv and Robert I. Lerman, "How Do Marital Status, Work Effort, and Wage Rates Interact?" *Demography* 44, no. 3 (August 2007): 624–47.

10. This information is taken from P. J. Huffstutter, "Town Faces Hazy Future after Exit of Auto Plant," *Los Angeles Times*, April 30, 2007.

11. Elijah Anderson, *Codes of the Street: Decency, Violence, and the Moral Life of the Inner City* (New York: Norton, 1999), 133–34.

12. Rick A. Mathews, Michael O. Maume, and William J. Miller, "Deindustrialization, Economic Distress, and Homicide Rates in Midsized Rustbelt Cities," *Homicide Studies* 5, no. 2 (2001): 83–113.

13. "Race, Ethnicity, and Health Care Fact Sheet," Henry J. Kaiser Family Foundation, July 2006.

14. For a more detailed analysis of the relationship between the economy, the growth of prisons, and higher education, see Jason Ziedenberg and Vincent Schiraldi, "Cell Blocks or Classrooms: The Funding of Higher Education and Corrections and Its Impact on African American Men," Justice Policy Institute Report, 2002, http://www.justicepolicy.org/coc1/corc.htm.

15. The information about Jasmine is taken from the video documentary "China Blue," produced by Teddy Bear Films, and directed by Micha X. Peled, 2006.

16. National Council of Textile Organizations, "U.S. Textile Industry," http://www.ncto.org/ustextiles/index.asp.

17. This information was taken from Wayne Tompkins, "Fruit of the Loom's Closing Tore at Fabric of Life in Campbellsville," and "Salvadorans Cling to Apparel Jobs," *Courier-Journal* (Louisville, KY), June 19, 2005, and June 19, 2005, respectively.

18. For a more detailed account of the plight of Chinese laborers under globalization and the particular exploitation of women in the process, see Pun Ngai, *Made in China: Women Factory Workers in a Global Workplace* (Durham, NC: Duke University Press, 2005).

19. "Human Development Report 2005: International Cooperation at a Crossroads; Aid, Trade and Security in an Unequal World," United Nations Development Program.

20. This description is taken from Robert Frank, "High-Paying U.S. Nanny Positions Puncture Fabric of Family Life in Developing Nations," *Wall Street Journal*, December 18, 2001.

21. Arlie Russell Hochschild, "Love and Gold," in *Global Woman: Nannies, Maids, and Sex Workers in the New Economy*, ed. Barbara Ehrenreich and Arlie Russell Hochschild (New York: Henry Holt, 2002), 20.

22. Rachel Salazar Parrenas, "The Care Crisis in the Philippines: Children and Transnational Families in the New Global Economy," in *Global Woman: Nannies, Maids, and Sex Workers in the New Economy*, ed. Barbara Ehrenreich and Arlie Russell Hochschild (New York: Henry Holt, 2002), 39–54.

23. Form I-140, United States Citizenship and Immigration Services, Department of Homeland Security.

24. Jeffrey S. Passel, "Estimates of the Size and Characteristics of the Undocumented Population," Pew Hispanic Center Report, March 2005.

6. VIOLENCE, SEX, AND POLITICS

1. Edward W. Said (1935–2003) was an influential English professor, social critic, and human rights activist.

2. Cited in Harold Herd, *The March of Journalism* (London: Allen and Unwin, 1952).

3. These examples are taken from Steven Starker's excellent historical review of controversies associated with the development of mass media: *Evil Influences: Crusades against the Mass Media* (New Brunswick, NJ: Transaction, 1989).

4. Quotes appeared in an article from the *Christian Spectator* (1822).

5. Representative Joe Baca, a Democrat representing California's Forty-third Congressional District.

6. "Generation M2: Media in the Lives of 8 to 18 Year Olds," Kaiser Family Foundation Study, 2010.

7. "Teens, Sex and TV" was jointly conducted by the Henry J. Kaiser Family Foundation and *US News and World Report*. It is a nationally representative sample of more than five hundred fifteen- to seventeen-year-olds.

8. Ryan G. Van Cleave, *Unplugged: My Journey into the Dark World of Video Game Addiction* (Deerfield Beach, FL: Health Communications, 2010).

9. The Tobacco Atlas, World Lung Foundation, 2012, http://tobaccoatlas.org/.

10. For details of this study, see Chris J. Boyatzis and Gina M. Matillo, "Effects of 'The Mighty Morphin Power Rangers' on Children's Aggression with Peers," *Child Study Journal* 25, no. 1 (1995): 45–55.

11. For details of this study, see R. H. DuRant, R. Neiberg, H. Champion, S. D. Rhodes, and M. Wolfson, "Viewing Professional Wrestling on Television and Engaging in Violent and Other Health Risk Behaviors," *Southern Medical Journal* 2 (2008): 129–37.

12. For a comprehensive review of this literature, see Steven J. Kirsh's excellent book *Children, Adolescents, and Media Violence*, 2nd ed. (Los Angeles: Sage, 2012).

13. Steven A. Kohm, Courtney A. Waid-Lindberg, Michael Weinrath, Tara O'Connor Shelley, and Rhonda R. Dobbs, "The Impact of Media on Fear of Crime among University Students: A Cross-National Comparison," *Canadian Journal of Criminology and Criminal Justice* 1 (2012): 67–100.

14. These figures are taken from a research summary posted by the Gallup organization: Jeffrey M. Jones, "Americans Still Perceive Crime as on the Rise," Gallup Politics,

November 18, 2010, http://www.gallup.com/poll/144827/americans-perceive-crime-rise.aspx.

15. Erin Hatton and Mary Nell Trautner, "Equal Opportunity Objectification? The Sexualization of Men and Women on the Cover of *Rolling Stone*," *Sexuality and Culture* 15 (2011): 256–78.

16. Neil Postman, *Amusing Ourselves to Death: Public Discourse in the Age of Show Business* (New York: Penguin, 1985), 73.

17. As reported by John Thorne in "Bouazizi Has Become a Tunisian Protest 'Symbol,'" *The National* (Abu Dhabi, United Arab Emirates), January 13, 2011.

7. FROM "ME" TO "WE"

1. Frederick Douglass was a former slave and leading abolitionist. This quote is taken from a speech he delivered on August 3, 1857, at Canandaigua, New York.

2. The account of the following events, including dialogue quotations, is taken from two sources: Rosa Parks (with Jim Haskins), *Rosa Parks: My Story* (New York: Penguin, 1992); and Douglas Brinkley, *Rosa Parks: A Life* (New York: Penguin, 2000).

3. John Conyers, congressman from Detroit, quoted in Monica Davey, "Two Sets of Park Memories: From Before the Boycott and After," *New York Times*, October 26, 2005.

4. For an excellent history and analysis of social movements, see Charles Tilly, *Social Movements, 1768–2004* (Boulder, CO: Paradigm, 2004).

5. Susan Zaeske has produced an extensive history of both petition gathering in the United States and the link between the abolitionist and feminist movements. See *Signatures of Citizenship: Petitioning, Antislavery, and Women's Political Identity* (Chapel Hill: University of North Carolina Press, 2003).

6. In some cases, the dispute panel will have four or five "judges," but the only way that a ruling can be rejected is if every single trade representative—all 152—agree to have the decision reversed.

7. For a more extensive history, analysis, and critique of neoliberalism, see David Harvey's *Brief History of Neoliberalism* (New York: Oxford University Press, 2005), and Naomi Klein's *Shock Doctrine: The Rise of Disaster Capitalism* (New York: Metropolitan Books, 2007).

8. The quote is from nonviolence trainer Matt Guynn and was reported by FAIR—the nonprofit news analysis organization. See FAIR's media advisory from December 7, 1999: "WTO Coverage: Prattle in Seattle."

9. As reported in FAIR, "WTO Coverage: Prattle in Seattle."

10. The focus of these demonstrations has included the WTO, IMF, World Bank, and G8. Crowd size is always difficult to determine, and the figures reported here are rough estimates based on averages of multiple media reports.

11. For an excellent review and analysis of the globalization movement, see Jeremy Brecher, Tim Costello, and Brendan Smith, *Globalization from Below: The Power of Solidarity* (Cambridge, MA: South End Press, 2002).

12. See John Nichols's firsthand account of the Wisconsin protests in his book *Uprising: How Wisconsin Renewed the Politics of Protest, from Madison to Wall Street* (New York: Nation Books, 2012).

13. For an insiders' perspective of the Wall Street protests, see *Occupying Wall Street: The Inside Story of an Action That Changed America* (New York: OR Books, 2011). This book was written in a collective voice by many of the leading activists who helped organize the Wall Street Occupation.

CONCLUSION

1. Peter Berger (born 1929) is an internationally recognized sociologist.

Index

About the Author

Peter L. Callero is professor of sociology at Western Oregon University where he teaches courses on community organizing, social theory, research methods, deviance, and the sociology of self. He holds a PhD in sociology from the University of Wisconsin–Madison and has published extensively on issues of self, identity, and politics. His other books are *Giving Blood: The Development of an Altruistic Identity* (with Jane Piliavin) and *The Self-Society Dynamic: Cognition, Emotion, and Action* (edited with Judith Howard).